SEE Change

Making the Transition to a Sustainable Enterprise Economy

SEE CHANGE

MAKING THE TRANSITION TO A
SUSTAINABLE ENTERPRISE ECONOMY

Sandra Waddock and **Malcolm McIntosh**

Greenleaf
PUBLISHING

© 2011 Greenleaf Publishing Limited

Published by Greenleaf Publishing Limited
Aizlewood's Mill
Nursery Street
Sheffield S3 8GG
UK
www.greenleaf-publishing.com

Printed in Great Britain on acid-free paper by
CPI Antony Rowe, Chippenham and Eastbourne

FSC
www.fsc.org
MIX
Paper from
responsible sources
FSC® C013604

Cover by LaliAbril.com

British Library Cataloguing in Publication Data:
   Waddock, Sandra A.
      Making the transition to a sustainable enterprise economy.
      -- (SEE change ; v. 1)
      1. Social responsibility of business. 2. Industries--
      Social aspects. 3. Industries--Environmental aspects.
      I. Title II. Series III. McIntosh, Malcolm, 1953-
      306.3-dc22

   ISBN-13: 9781906093457

This book is for all those people working for the development of the sustainable enterprise economy—difference makers in the world: whatever their position and status, those people who care about social justice, sustainability and peace for us humans and all the other creatures that share our beautiful planet.

Contents

Abbreviations

AAFP	American Academy of Family Physicians
ABA	American Beverage Association
BALLE	Business Alliance for Local Living Economies
BoP	bottom-of-the-pyramid/base-of-the pyramid
BRIC	Brazil, Russia, India, China
CC	corporate citizenship
CCL	Centre for Creative Leadership (US)
CR	corporate responsibility
CSO	civil society organisation
CSR	corporate social responsibility
EABIS	European Academy for Business in Society
EIA	Energy Information Administration
ESG	environmental, social and governance [goals]
ESOP	employee share ownership plan
FAO	Food and Agriculture Organisation
GAN	global action network
GDP	Gross Domestic Product
GNP	Gross National Product
GPI	Genuine Progress Indicator
GRI	Global Reporting Initiative
HPI	Happy Planet Index
IEA	International Energy Agency
IMF	International Monetary Fund
IPCC	Intergovernmental Panel on Climate Change
MDG	Millennium Development Goal
MFI	micro-finance institution
MNC	multinational corporation
NGO	non-governmental organisation
NIC	National Intelligence Council (US)
PACI	Partnering Against Corruption Initiative
SRI	socially responsible investment
TI	Transparency International
UNDP	UN Development Programme
UNEP	UN Environment Programme
WBCSD	World Business Council for Sustainable Development
WHO	World Health Organisation
WTO	World Trade Organisation
WWF	World Wide Fund for Nature

Foreword

James E. Post

Do you believe that human beings are on a collision course with planet Earth?

Do you doubt that we are on the pathway of unsustainable resource consumption and waste production that guarantees our children and grandchildren will have a poorer life than we have today—in other words, that the feared downward spiral has begun.

Do you wonder whether anyone is awake to these challenges and capable of offering practical suggestions as to how human systems might alter, or reverse, damaging behaviours?

If you have answered affirmatively to these questions, there is a good chance that you are already committed to generating more knowledge and more action to build a sustainable enterprise economy. And, if you are so committed, this book is for you.

Strategic thinkers have the gift of looking at the world and being able to frame, focus and define the most complex problems in comprehensible, action-oriented terms. Sandra Waddock and Malcolm McIntosh have written a book that frames the issues, focuses the mind on what matters most, and defines where we need to go as a human beings with conscience, intelligence and courage. Their strategic view rests on an impressive body of scientific knowledge and practical wisdom.

Scenarios of the future

As we look to the future, there is a rapidly growing and considerable knowledge of the realities that almost certainly await the planet and its people in the 21st century. This enables us to think in terms of scenarios of what may lie ahead and prepare for the consequences of the decisions we make.

As shown in Figure 1, the two great drivers of change seem to be (a) human readiness to act (low to high) in response to (b) the knowledge we are prepared to accept (ranging from old paradigms to new theories). If we continue to adhere to old theories and knowledge while simultaneously displaying little readiness to act, we seem destined to live a scenario of paralysis and degradation (quadrant A). A second possibility is adherence to old knowledge, theories and models, with the caveat that a paradigm might happen under extraordinary circumstances (quadrant B). This scenario reminds us that 'black swan' events do happen.[1]

Figure 1 **Four scenarios**

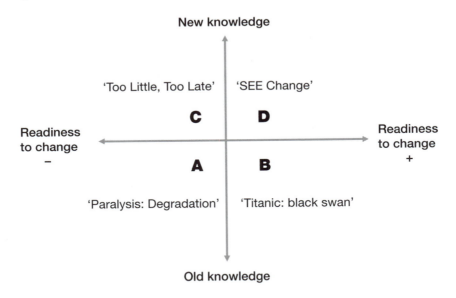

---

1   This scenario is named in honour of the distinguished sailor E.J. Smith who, before he took the HMS *Titanic* on its maiden voyage into a fierce black-swan-like night in April 1912, said he 'could not imagine any condition which would cause the ship to founder'.

Quadrant C describes contemporaries who accept accumulating new knowledge, but refuse to act on it by changing their own behaviour in significant and meaningful ways. Too many collective bodies—governments, companies—seem to be stuck in this morass, mouthing commitment to sustainability goals but adhering to unsustainable ways. The fourth quadrant (quadrant D) is where Waddock and McIntosh place their hope. Mounting evidence in the physical, natural and social sciences will move leaders and the public past the tipping point toward a sustainable enterprise economy ('SEE Change').

Can a revolution happen?

The early months of 2011 brought a new reality to the lives of people in the Middle East and North Africa. After decades of political suppression and economic and social desperation, a spark of revolution took hold, first in Tunisia, then Egypt, Libya, Yemen, Jordan, Bahrain and other nations. In a few weeks, the fire of freedom spread across the whole of the region. It is too early to know where these revolutions will end. But, for a time, the unthinkable has happened as the world has looked on in wonder.

Revolutions do happen. Economic and political transformation is possible. The events of 2011 remind even the most sceptical among us that great changes are within the imagination and grasp of human beings.

The pathway to a sustainable enterprise economy is filled with challenges—technological, political, social and economic. Some are challenges of the mind, but the most formidable are the challenges of the spirit. Hope is rooted in faith: in this case, the faith that human beings have the intelligence to embrace new theories and knowledge, and the readiness to do the work that will make this revolution—this *SEE Change*—a reality. Impossible? One need look to the events of 2011 in North Africa and the Middle East to find a reason to believe.

James E. Post, March 2011

Preface

Turning and turning in the widening gyre
The falcon cannot hear the falconer;
Things fall apart; the centre cannot hold;
Mere anarchy is loosed upon the world,
The blood-dimmed tide is loosed, and everywhere
The ceremony of innocence is drowned;
The best lack all conviction, while the worst
Are full of passionate intensity.

William Butler Yeats, 'The Second Coming'

We can find no better words to express our dismay with the state of the world today than these immortal words from William Butler Yeats' great poem 'The Second Coming'. Indeed, it sometimes seems that in the face of a catastrophic economic meltdown, with potentially disastrous effects of climate change imminent, ecological systems all around us in danger of collapsing, and enormous inequities in the distribution of wealth and resources in the world that optimism is hard to come by. The world seems to be fast crumbling around us, yet we are reminded by Yeats and by a sense of history that we have faced difficult times before and come through them.

The problem, as we see it, is that this time there may not be another chance unless we can find the 'passionate intensity' among the best of us to act proactively and constructively in the face of seemingly insurmountable obstacles. We believe that the systems on which the world is organised need to change and change dramatically to face the eventually unavoidable realities that nature combined with humanity press upon us.

The imperatives that lay claim on us to change are many and seemingly too few can find the courage and conviction to act on what, in their hearts, they know to be the right things to do.

Despite this discouragement, we are hopeful. Thus, we have tried to write a hopeful and optimistic book that highlights not only what needs to change in our world, but also and importantly how that change is already beginning to happen. In what follows we outline a framework that we call SEE Change—the change to a sustainable enterprise economy—and detail the ways in which that change is already emerging.

We cannot say that SEE Change will happen quickly enough or with enough impact to effect the changes that will be needed to bring humanity into symbiosis with our 'ground', the natural environment that supports us. But we are optimistic that there are many, many entrepreneurs already acting in constructive ways and in many different types of enterprise, ranging from traditional and very large businesses to small start-up social ventures. It is well within the capacity of inspired humans, who find meaning and energy in their work, to change the world. And we hope that this book inspires that many more such sustainable enterprise entrepreneurs and difference makers to act.

Sandra Waddock   *Malcolm McIntosh*
Boston, USA   *Brisbane, Australia*
December 2010

1
The context for SEEing change

The world is beset with problems . . . so many that they sometimes seem insurmountable. And some, such as climate change, global inequities, resource and ecological collapse, can be classed as emergencies requiring urgent and immediate action. We need real and lasting change—what we call in this book *SEE Change*—a systemic transition to an emerging sustainable enterprise economy[1] which is now being undertaken by many institutions, enterprises and collectivities in the world's social, political, financial and ecological systems.

The emerging part, of course, is whether the change will be big and soon enough to make a difference, so devastating and deep are some of the problems we face. Indeed, it can be discouraging even to recount the many ways in which the human species is failing our planet. In this book, although we do begin with an overview of some of the major issues (all of which, it could be argued, humanity has created for itself), we ultimately want to try to paint a more optimistic picture. We believe that enterprises of all sorts, business enterprises included, can and *need* to be sources of innovation, creativity and sensibility.

---

1 The subtitle of this book is inspired by Karl Polanyi's classic book *The Great Transformation: The Political and Economic Origins of Our Times* (Boston, MA: Beacon Press, reprinted 2001).

SEE Change will be difficult but, as we hope to illustrate, the seeds of change in all sectors, and in new and fundamentally different forms, are already being planted and beginning to grow. However, the core problem is that we, as humans, need to learn to 'see' in new ways in order to create a sufficiently broad, coherent and integrated social movement for change that can overturn the momentum of the current system. Basically, we need to recognise that change at the system level, not just incremental change, is needed. Change is needed in our financial structures and systems, in what we value and do not value in our economic systems, and in the many human systems and organisations that we have conceived, developed and implemented. Deep change is needed in the purposing, goals and practice of business enterprise. Change is needed in the ways that we, as humans, relate to nature and natural systems, most of which are under severe stress from resource overuse and depletion, the strains of a quadrupled population during the 20th century, and human impacts on climate. And change is needed in the ways in which we relate to each other, use our time and build our communities.

Thus, we can think about SEE Change in a number of ways that relate to the 'SEE Change' title that frames this book and with which this chapter will deal. First, there is the capacity to actually 'see' the changes that are needed—what we believe are big and important changes in the ways in which society organises itself with respect to planetary resources. Thus SEE Change is about systemic change within the whole of society that affects businesses and other enterprises, that creates new organisational models and partnerships (and crosses old boundaries), and that uses the new technological capacities and attendant transparencies to create new pressures that can potentially democratise societies and their enterprises in a real way.

There are, of course, dangers and risks associated with this type of transformation, because no one can predict the actual outcomes or full implications of significant and potentially disruptive system change. Yet, as we can already see, and as this chapter will detail, there is a clear need for change if humanity is not to create untenable conditions for our grandchildren to live in. Thus, what we really need is a 'sea change'—change that focuses on going beyond 'sustainability' with its implications of maintaining (literally, sustaining) what already currently exists. We really need to move towards thriving, not simply sustaining, societies and enterprises for the many, not just the few. And the definition of 'many' in this context needs to encompass not just human beings but also the other species that live with us on Earth, inextricably bound together in what Fritjof Capra calls the web of life (Capra 1995).

We believe that a move to SEE—the sustainable enterprise economy—is imperative. Humanity needs a sustainable enterprise *economy*, filled with sustainable enterprises of all sorts, and based on significantly different economic imperatives than today's growth-oriented, profit-maximising, rich-get-richer incentives. The question is: how do we move to this SEE Change in light of the many obstacles to change and in the face of significant climatic, economic and social disruptions that have now become evident. In this chapter, we will discuss the current conditions and then highlight both 'top down' change from existing (and frequently large) institutions, such as multinational corporations, and 'bottom up' change from new types of enterprises that are beginning to be established with multiple-bottom-line orientations.

Underlying these descriptions is a sense that no single theory of change or, indeed, practice of change, will effect needed transformations in the economic, social and political spheres. We believe that we will need change coming simultaneously from many different directions, taking numerous and varied forms. In this and the next chapter we will illustrate how some of that change is already under way.

The Global Compact

Since 2000, the UN Global Compact[2] has been building what it now claims is the largest corporate citizenship organisation in the world, with more than 8,000 signatories, of which nearly 5,300 are companies. Signatories pledge to uphold the Global Compact's ten basic principles around human rights, labour rights, sustainability and anti-corruption. But the Global Compact, and many related initiatives, are but a small aspect of the changes that are needed to move us to a sustainable enterprise economy. Management thinker Peter Senge has called the move to sustainability a 'necessary revolution' that we are now beginning to live through (Senge *et al.* 2008). Just how significant is the UN Global Compact in the scale of things? And how might it make a greater contribution to facing the future?

---

2   For further information on the Global Compact see www.unglobalcompact.org.

The Global Compact sits within the ambit of an emerging and still voluntary global governance framework, with the aim of humanising business at its core. Along with a number of other important new social partnerships that have evolved in the last 20 years, the Global Compact's fundamental purpose is to try to civilise the market and globalisation process. Some would say that its fundamental purpose is to bring *people* back into the picture (see below). In the speech that ultimately led to the establishment of the UN Global Compact, the then UN Secretary-General Kofi Annan called for a new 'social compact of shared values and principles, which will give a human face to the global market' (Annan 1999). Basically, it serves also as one of many efforts to bring balance back to the relationship between people and planet.

People, planet, wellbeing and enterprise

While there has been great use of the concept 'people, planet and prosperity' to describe sustainable development, the 2008 crisis in global capitalism has helped shift the focus not simply to financial prosperity but much more importantly to wellbeing. The evidence is straightforward and has been well documented (Csikszentmihalyi 1999): economic success does not necessarily equate to happiness or wellbeing. Further, the rolling housing, financial and company collapses beginning in 2008 vividly illustrate that an excess of competition and financial wealth can lead to social instability and breakdown, a tearing of the social fabric that might otherwise bind people together.

The combined global economic, climate and social crises have arguably created an inflection point that makes *now* the time to start moving towards thinking conceptually about wellbeing, rather than growth, as the fundamental value to be embedded both in society and economy. For some this issue, though uncomfortable, can lead to rethinking our relationships, both to each other and to the planet.

The climate change conundrum

Early in the 21st century an international scientific consensus concluded that humanity was significantly contributing to the destruction of life on Earth (IPCC 2007). The Intergovernmental Panel on Climate Change (IPCC) concluded that the evidence on climate change (sometimes termed 'global warming') was 'unequivocal', with attendant rising of sea levels, decreases in snow and ice, shifting weather patterns, and serious and potentially catastrophic impacts on natural systems to be expected. The cause—greenhouse gases emitted by human activities, attributable to industrialisation processes and population growth.

In the wake of 9/11 British Prime Minister, Tony Blair, and his Chief Scientific Advisor, Professor David King, said that climate change was an even greater global threat than terrorism.[3]

Climate change and the state of nature

The 2007 IPCC report and Al Gore's movie *An Inconvenient Truth* (both Nobel Peace Prize winners in 2007), along with numerous books and reports on the subject, have made climate change the subject of popular attention globally. It is hard to open a magazine or newspaper today without the issue appearing front and centre. But while climate change may be the *issue* that captured the attention of the many who are becoming more vulnerable to its effects, one third of the world's population are vulnerable to its effects, living in a state of want and fear, without the bare necessities of life. Climate change adds another layer to the challenges that nearly three billion people face every day confronting starvation, poverty, violence, exploitation, discrimination and disease.

Some statistics from the IPCC report of 2007 and the 2009 Conference of the Parties in Copenhagen (IPCC 2007) make interesting—and frightening—reading. For example, atmospheric concentration levels of carbon dioxide, the most important of the greenhouse gases, now vastly surpass anything that can be measured over the past 650,000 years, based on analysis of ice cores. The IPCC attributes this increase in carbon dioxide to fossil fuels and shifts in land usage, with simultaneous increases in methane gases, attributable to agriculture and fossil fuels. Other important shifts include increasing average Arctic temperatures and shrinking Arctic sea ice, noticeable changes in precipitation amounts, with significantly greater precipitation in eastern North and South America, northern Europe and central Asia, and decreased precipitation in the Sahel, the Mediterranean, southern Africa and some of southern Asia. The latter has led to longer and more severe droughts in parts of the world, with noticeable changes

---

3 www.ipcc.ch/publications_and_data/ar4/syr/en/main.html.

in extreme temperatures, meaning fewer cold days and nights, less frost and more frequent heat waves, as well as an observed increase in tropical cyclone activity. The IPCC concludes that: 'Discernible human influences now extend to other aspects of the climate, including ocean warming, continental-average temperatures, temperature extremes and wind patterns' (IPCC 2007: 10).

More recent data from the Worldwatch Institute's Vital Signs study suggests that although there was a slight cooling of global temperatures in 2008, carbon dioxide emissions and concentrations in the atmosphere continue to rise and were 2% up in 2008 compared to 2007. Despite lower per capita emissions in the developing world than in the developed world, China's rapidly emerging economy has created a situation in which carbon emissions per capita are still increasing at a rate of 6% per year (Mulrow 2009). Worldwatch has also issued a guide to climate change that details how different parts of the world are likely to be affected. For example, North America faces the possibility of greater fire risk and more deaths from heatwaves. South America could experience declines in glacier melt that threaten drinking and agricultural water supplies, the replacement of tropical forests by savannahs and massive extinctions in tropical regions, combined with lower crop and livestock yields. Europe could face coastal flooding and flash floods inland, species extinctions, less productive crops and increased heatwaves, while in Asia over a billion people may be at risk from reduced freshwater supplies and affected by decreased crop yields. Asia potentially faces rising mortality from diarrhoeal disease and cholera, flooding, and loss of coral reefs and mangroves, while Australia and New Zealand could suffer from lack of fresh water, droughts and flooding in coastal regions. In Africa somewhere between 75 and 250 million people could lack fresh water by 2020, crops could be severely reduced and flooding could occur in delta regions where there is heavy population (McKeown and Gardners 2009).

Human civilisation will be affected, sometimes dramatically, by these climate changes—and more are expected if global warming continues unabated. Further, although many scientists believe that human action can slow climate change, the IPCC strongly notes that because of the slow response of oceans to changes, global warming and rising sea levels associated with it are likely to continue for centuries even if significant action were to be taken immediately.

Beyond climate change

There are serious ecological problems that go well beyond climate change.[4] Let us consider some of these issues. One in four species of large mammals is already in danger of extinction as a result of habitat loss and hunting, causing serious disruption to food chains, and ultimately affecting human beings as well. The oceans of the world are sick, with one study counting more than 150 'dead zones' that range from less than a square mile to up to 45,000 square miles. The numbers of these dead zones have been doubling in number every decade since the 1960s. Very few species live in dead zones because of a lack of oxygen in the water, a problem that is likely to be made worse by global warming.[5] Fisheries pose a problem too, with nearly all major fish stocks in danger of collapse by the mid-21st century (Worm *et al.* 2006).

The Amazon's rainforests are also in danger, with one estimate by the World Wide Fund for Nature (WWF) indicating that as many as half of them could be destroyed or badly damaged by as early as 2030 (Nepstad 2008). Because everything in the natural environment is linked, such massive destruction of rainforest could exacerbate global warming and change rainfall patterns throughout the world. To further complicate matters, polar sea ice is melting at unprecedented rates, raising fears of rising sea levels and an irreversible loss of the snowcap that is partially responsible for maintaining the Earth's equilibrium at levels that sustain humanity.

Although there is evidence that poorer nations will be more adversely affected by climate change than richer ones, one recent study by Richard Tol (Tol 2009: 44) suggests that current estimates of the economic impact of climate may not be particularly useful because there are too many missing variables in current analyses. For example, there is considerable uncertainty about social costs potentially associated with climate change, and these costs may be seriously underestimated in many studies, especially because they contain only readily quantifiable impacts. Further, although some models suggest that climate change could for some countries or regions even have short-term beneficial effects, there are many effects that have not been included in previous studies. These missing effects

4 A good synopsis of these issues can be found on the EarthFirst website: earthfirst. com/7-environmental-problems-that-are-worse-than-we-thought, accessed 13 January 2009.

5 '150 "Dead Zones" Counted in Oceans', 29 March 2004, www.msnbc.msn.com/ id/4624359, accessed 13 January 2009.

include saltwater intrusion into groundwater, higher water temperatures, more 'extratropical' storms (although higher winds could in fact lessen wind-energy costs). But, as Tol (2009: 44) points out, these unknowns 'pale in comparison to the big unknowns: extreme climate scenarios, the very long-term biodiversity loss, the possible effects of climate change on economic development, and even political violence'.

We could go on, but we have made the point that the natural environment has suffered at humankind's hands. More importantly, since the late 1980s humanity has been in what the Global Footprint Network calls 'ecological overshoot'.[6] Ecological overshoot is the condition in which humanity uses more natural resources than the earth can regenerate, creating a sort of naturalistic deficit. Indeed, the Global Footprint Network claims that we now need 1.5 Earths simply to support humanity at current levels of consumption (and hence are in deficit spending), with many impoverished populations still striving to attain developed-country levels of consumption. It is important to note that, according to levels of consumption, around one third of the human population requires about one planet equivalent and about 20% require between two and four planets, including most people in North America, Europe and Australia.

Inequity and poverty

Global inequity and poverty remain highly problematic, despite some movement towards partial achievement of some of the UN's Millennium Development Goals. In 2008, the World Bank estimated that some 1.4 billion people live at or below a poverty line of the equivalent of US$1.25 per day, up from an earlier estimate of one billion at the poverty line, and almost half the world lives on less than US$2.50 per day.[7] Although this figure represents a drop of about 25% in the incidence of poverty, when accounting for population growth much of the reduction came about because of China's economic growth. Inequity—the gap between rich and poor—continues to be rife with the wealthiest 20% of the global population

---

6 www.footprintnetwork.org/en/index.php/GFN/page/2010_living_planet_report, accessed 16 December 2010).

7 The World Bank revised the poverty line from US$1 to US$1.25 to conform to better data. For more details, see Anup Sha, *Poverty Around the World*, www.globalissues.org/article/4/poverty-around-the-world, accessed 9 January 2008.

consuming nearly 80% of global resources. In its revised estimates, the World Bank notes that because earlier calculations had underestimated the cost of living in developing countries, there are actually higher poverty rates than past data have indicated.[8]

Further, studies of the impact of climate change on developed and developing nations suggest that it is developing nations that are likely to be hurt the most, despite the fact that the per capita ecological footprint is considerably higher in developed nations (Tol 2009). The Human Development Report of 2007–2008 suggests that more than 80% of people now live in countries where the gap between rich and poor is becoming worse (Watkins 2008). The Global Issues website notes the following facts associated with poverty and inequity in today's world:[9]

- Some 25,000 children die daily from the effects of poverty (e.g. malnutrition, poor sanitation, poor health);

- Of the world's 6.7 billion people, nearly a billion are unable to read or write;

- Some 1.1 billion lack access to clean water;

- 2.6 billion lack basic sanitation;

- Nearly half of the 2.2 billion children in the world live in poverty, of which 640 million have inadequate shelter, and 400 million do not have clean water; and

- Some 15 million children are estimated to be orphaned because of HIV/AIDS.

Further, in the west, the gap between rich and poor has grown rapidly over the past few decades. A study by the Federal Reserve Survey of Consumer Finances published in 2009 showed that the wealthiest 1% of the population in the US controlled nearly 34% of the wealth, while the next 9% controlled 28.5%, leaving the bottom 90% to share just 37.3% of total wealth. The 400 people listed in the *Forbes* annual ranking of America's

---

8 www.globalissues.org/article/4/poverty-around-the-world#WorldBanksPoverty EstimatesRevised, accessed 11 December 2009.

9 www.globalissues.org/article/26/poverty-facts-and-stats#src4, accessed 11 December 2009. This website carries much more information about poverty, climate change and related issues.

richest people, collectively held more than 2% of the country's wealth.[10] A US Congressional Budget Office survey, released in 2009, shows similar disparities in income distribution, with the top 20% receiving nearly 56% of income in the US, and the bottom 20% only about 4%.[11]

Terrorism, violence and conflict

Terrorism, violence and conflict are other realities that modern enterprises must face, particularly in the globalised economy. Although many people believe that terrorism is connected to poverty, recent evidence suggests that may not be the case. Indeed, two recent studies find no relationship between terrorism and poverty. One study by James Piazza found that there was no relationship between indicators of economic development (which included per capita income, GDP, prices, employment and food security) and terrorism (Piazza 2006: 170). Instead, Piazza found that social and cultural stratification, ethnic and religious diversity, repression by governments, and 'political systems with large, complex, multiparty systems' experienced more terrorism than their opposites (Piazza 2006: 171). These findings were confirmed by Alberto Abadie (2006: 51) who found no relationship between terrorism and poorer nations when political freedom and other country-specific indicators were included. Abadie identifies a U-shaped relationship between political freedom and terrorism, with countries with moderate levels of freedom experiencing more than either repressive or very free nations. Indeed this research is supported by the Happy Planet Index from the New Economics Foundation (to which we return in Chapter 2) which shows that it is possible to have high levels of life satisfaction and life expectancy with relatively low levels of financial wealth and low carbon footprints.

Business enterprise, however, is implicated in terrorism because for some observers it seems that the growth of globalisation is an underlying factor in fostering terrorism. As Matthew Morgan puts it (2004: 36):

---

10 www.toomuchonline.org/inequality.html, accessed 15 December 2009. The full study can be found at www.federalreserve.gov/Pubs/feds/2009/200913/200913abs.html.

11 www.cbo.gov/ftpdocs/100xx/doc10068/effective_tax_rates_2006.pdf, accessed 15 December 2009.

> The process of globalisation, which involves the technologi-
> cal, political, economic, and cultural diminution of boundaries
> between countries across the world, has insinuated a self-in-
> terested, inexorable, corrupting market culture into traditional
> communities. Many see these forces as threatening their way of
> life. At the same time that globalisation has provided a motiva-
> tion for terrorism, it has also facilitated methods for it.

Morgan goes on to highlight some of the factors that are associated with
the rise of what he terms 'new terrorism', which he claims poses unprecedented threats. These factors include culture, particularly culture associated with fundamentalist religious views, the rise of personality-driven
cults, and the religious right in the US, with many religiously motivated
terrorists believing that their violence is morally justified. There are also
political and organisational factors, such as the intrusion of Western values on non-Western nations and, as noted above, processes of globalisation themselves, associated with terrorism (Morgan 2004: 37). Ironically,
the very elements of globalisation that modern enterprise has developed
for its own uses, such as communications and other technologies, make
terrorism more dangerous than ever. Global communications technologies and other factors are reducing boundaries, enabling instantaneous
communications globally, and assuring rapid transport, not to mention
advanced weaponry. As Morgan notes (2004: 38):

> Among the factors that contribute to this are the easing of bor-
> der controls and the development of globe-circling infrastruc-
> tures, which support recruitment, fund-raising, movement of
> material, and other logistical functions.

Energy

Energy use has been at the heart of human development over millennia.
Today, issues of energy production and use affect rich and poor: the poor
because of their reliance on locally sourced wood and coal; and the rich
because of their wasteful addiction to easy energy produced, in the main,
from fossil fuels. According to the International Energy Agency (IEA),
about 34% of the world's energy supply in 2006 came from non-renewable

oil resources, while another 20.5% is from gas.[12] Further, energy demand is expected to continue to grow as population expands, with the US Energy Information Administration predicting a 50% increase in demand from 2005 projected to 2030. Much of that increase is expected to come from non-OECD countries of the developing world, as they strive to reach developed nation status.[13]

Developed countries consume considerably more energy resources on a per capita basis than do developing nations, with the US at 5% of global population alone consuming 25% of the world's energy resources, roughly comparable to the 30% of energy used by the developing countries combined.[14] Peak oil, which is the peak of the Earth's oil production or extraction, is a controversial topic. However, the Association for the Study of Peak Oil and Gas estimates that the peak of discovering oil occurred sometime in the 1960s, while consumption overshot new discoveries in 1981.[15] All of this in a world where the US Energy Department estimates that some 2 billion people are without access to electricity, with the US using about 15 times more energy per capita than people in developing nations.[13]

Claiming that the global energy system is at a crossroads and that trends in energy consumption are patently unsustainable, the IEA says that current consumption patterns must be altered (IEA 2008). The IEA used scenario analysis to study different possible futures for the use of energy, and found that whatever alternative sources of energy are developed, the world is likely to continue to rely on oil for many years. In reaching this conclusion, the IEA states boldly that: 'Preventing catastrophic and irreversible damage to the global climate ultimately requires a major decarbonisation of the world energy sources' (IEA 2008: 3) Further, the IEA expects that if their economic growth continues, more than half of the increase in energy demand will come from India and China before 2030. Although the projections suggest there is enough oil and gas supply to support rising demand until 2030, reserves of both are concentrated in a

---

12 International Energy Agency, www.iea.org/textbase/nppdf/free/2008/key_stats_2008.pdf, accessed 9 May 2009.

13 Energy Information Administration, www.eia.doe.gov/oiaf/ieo/world.html, accessed 9 May 2009.

14 Solar Energy International, www.solarenergy.org/resources/energyfacts.html, accessed 9 May 2009.

15 Association for the Study of Peak Oil and Gas, www.peakoil.net/about-peak-oil, accessed 9 May 2009.

financial capital; manufactured capital; natural capital; social capital; and human capital.

Investors, of course, use traditional forms of financial capital in their investments, but some, typically called social, responsibility or ethical investors, are also concerned about ESG issues and invest with these considerations in mind. Additionally, resource scarcity and the need to account for externalities not taken into consideration in traditional accounting approaches has many corporate critics seeking forms of life-cycle or full-cost accounting that do take into account the real costs of producing goods and services. However many forms of capital are ultimately determined to be relevant to business success, it is beginning to become clearer that more forms than simply financial capital need to be taken into account if businesses are to sustain their social legitimacy.

The large corporation and SEE Change

Sustainable enterprise can be conceived as operating on the basis of the ten UN Global Compact principles,[7] which collectively deal with human rights, labour rights, sustainability and anti-corruption. To these ten we would add principles of peace, equity and social justice. Some companies that are attempting to act more sustainably are recognised, for example, in listings such as the Global 100 Sustainable Companies, published annually by Corporate Knights and Innovest Strategic Value Advisors (now part of MSCI, Inc.), or the numerous other rankings that now exist as part of the growing infrastructure that attempts to pressure companies towards more responsible practices.

Rankings work by making visible the leaders (and excluding the laggards), and by highlighting key issues of interest (e.g. sustainability, supply chain management, human rights). They also bring the performance of companies on those and related practices (or lack thereof) to light. Some companies, such as Cisco Systems, Intel, Google and even General Electric (especially with its Ecomagination programme), consistently appear in rankings such as Barron's World's Most Respected Companies, Fortune's Most Admired Companies and others that highlight specific topics.

As an example, among the US companies that appeared in *Newsweek* 2010 'green' rankings were (in order): Dell, Hewlett-Packard, IBM, Johnson

---

7 www.unglobalcompact.org.

& Johnson and Intel. The top five on The Global 100 were IBM, Hewlett-Packard, Johnson & Johnson, Sony and GlaxoSmithKline.[8] Many NGOs, activists and pressure groups would claim that each of these companies has problematic practices—and they would certainly be correct. The point of rankings such as *Newsweek*'s (and the many others that have proliferated in recent years) is not to declare perfection in companies, because as large human enterprises, they are unlikely *ever* to achieve that status. Rather, it is to highlight state-of-the-art practices around issues such as sustainability, working conditions, employment for women and minorities, reputation and leadership. Such rankings also highlight the best work that is currently being done with the hope of engendering a constructive 'race-to-the-top' attitude so that companies will compete to perform better on these ESG issues.

Responsible enterprises deliver value to all stakeholders while not externalising costs onto the natural environment or society. Ultimately, since no large business currently meets this rather high standard (although some, like the carpet manufacturer Interface, and a few others, have committed themselves to doing so), this concept involves a significant redesign of the nature and purpose of enterprise itself.

Putting the needs of societies and a broad array of stakeholders on a par with, or even ahead of, the needs of shareholders would, we believe, give capitalism a more 'human' and equitable face, with companies finding themselves more sustainable—ecologically, socially and, importantly, economically. We both admit, however, to being somewhat sceptical that large corporations, under the current system, can effect sufficient systemic change to become sustainable. As we will explore in the next section, however, there are initiatives under way to try to 'reform' the corporation so that it better meets today's needs. We also believe that some (perhaps much) of what is going on in the name of sustainability may, in fact, be mere window dressing, 'green-washing' or 'just PR', as many critics claim. Yet it is also clear that significant change has begun in some very progressive companies, despite the many paradoxes and tensions that they face in moving towards greater sustainability and responsibility. Below we will explore some of the shifts that are currently evident.

---

8 www.newsweek.com/feature/2010/green-rankings.html, accessed 22 December 2010.

Box 1 **BMW**

Part of the automobile industry, which is still highly dependent on oil-based energy and other non-renewable resources, BMW has nonetheless taken an industry lead in the area of sustainability. Back in 2000, the company's Board of Directors declared sustainability to be one of the company's core strategic principles. The company's sustainability strategy ranges from the development of fuel-saving and alternative vehicle concepts to clean production processes and waste recycling programmes.[9] In 2009, BMW announced that it would dedicate significant new resources to the development of new drive technologies and projects in the field of sustainability. BMW also ensures that 95% of the components that it uses on its vehicles can be recycled later on. According to its *Sustainability Value Report 2008*, BMW's major areas of action with respect to sustainability are product responsibility, group-wide environmental protection, employees and society. BMW has been recognised for its accomplishments. In 2009 it topped the Dow Jones Sustainability Index for the automobile sector.[10]

Extended enterprises

What we often think of as traditional corporations, even very large multinational corporations, have changed significantly in recent years. Many have drastically altered to become much flatter in structure and therefore less hierarchical structurally, and some have even evolved into network organisations with very little of the actual production being done within the parent company. Simultaneously, especially since the mid-1990s, many large companies have implemented significant CR and sustainability programmes that have, at least to a small extent, begun to reshape their societal roles and impacts. Companies with a high public profile have, in particular, adopted CR platforms, developed codes of conduct for themselves, their suppliers and distributors, and made initial efforts to think about (ecological) sustainability or 'greening'. They have done so partly to protect their corporate brand or product/service brands, partly

9 www.bmwgroup.com/responsibility.
10 www.sustainability-indexes.com.

to respond to stakeholder concerns and partly to address the demands of the growing responsibility infrastructure.

The extended supply and distribution chains that now effectively constitute some companies represent a significant reshaping of corporations. For example, many large companies now form extended supply and distribution networks in which affiliated (but not owned) companies are subcontracted or outsourced to undertake actual production processes. The headquarters of these firms, which include many footwear, electronics, clothing and toy companies, serves more as a design/marketing vehicle and coordinator of 'independent' but linked suppliers and distributors than as a manager of units within a single entity. Many footwear companies, such as Nike and Reebok, have no manufacturing facilities of their own. Instead, they simply outsource all of their production, keeping design and brand management in house. Much the same can be said of most clothing firms. These companies have had to learn tough lessons since the mid-1990s, when stakeholder activists discovered abusive practices of all sorts in their suppliers' facilities—and did not let the outsourcing and highly branded company off the responsibility hook for these practices.

These so-called 'extended enterprises' (Post, Preston and Sachs 2002a, 2002b) are frequently held together by a shared strategic vision and common production goals, and sometimes by a common set of values articulated through codes of conduct and other mechanisms. They become stakeholders to each other in ways that are relatively new because they need to collaborate closely with internal as well as external stakeholders. They can be enormously complex to navigate and their boundaries are fuzzy, which can cause problems to those who want to hold them to account for what happens in their supply networks. Sometimes, however, the linkages among the elements of a network are quite tenuous, such as when headquartered companies contract with manufacturing facilities in developing nations to actually produce the goods that they sell and then those contractors subcontract again to other, even smaller companies or manufacturers. Still, depending on the nature of the firm and what is being produced, there may also be electronic connectivity and sometimes even equipment, functions and people shared among companies within an extended enterprise. For example, the logistics of orders and raw materials, production and shipment can be closely coordinated among units in the extended enterprise, making it difficult to be exactly sure where one enterprise ends and another begins.

In the early days these outsourced supply- and distribution-chain contracts tended to be arms-length relationships, in which companies simply subcontracted for what they needed without giving much thought to how and under what conditions the goods were actually produced. They are still pretty much arm's-length for many companies that do not have brand reputations to protect; however, there is increased pressure even on these companies (which tend to supply branded companies in any case) to improve their performance, with pressure often coming from the branded companies themselves. Starting in the 1990s, pressure groups, activists and NGOs began raising a public outcry against some of the working, environmental and labour rights abuses in subcontracting factories. Unsatisfied with the hands-off stance, they wanted to know what the parent or contracting company was going to do about these problems, even if they were not directly of the company's 'own' making. Responses like the one that then Nike CEO Phil Knight gave—that it was essentially not Nike's problem because the factories were not owned by Nike—further raised critics' hackles. It soon became clear that multinationals needed to ensure that suppliers' working, labour and environmental conditions met their own company's standards if the company was not to receive significant negative publicity—and sometimes even consumer boycotts, such as Nike faced in the late 1990s.

The problems with labour, environmental and human rights abuses in some supplier companies in developing nations created a context in which, as part of their corporate citizenship, many companies began to ask suppliers to live up to their own corporate codes of conduct. Sometimes, when companies are particularly in the spotlight, they even send their own employees to monitor factory conditions. The most progressive companies, bowing to the growing pressure from the responsibility infrastructure and activists, sometimes hire independent agencies to audit and certify that practices in manufacturing facilities meet the company's codes and standards, and that no labour or other abuses exist. While these auditing and certification programmes are not without their problems, they represent a significant advance beyond the hands-off approaches of earlier days.

Corporate citizenship as we know it today grew up in this context of changing corporate structures, intense global competition, increasing globalisation and a growth-at-all-costs mentality, as a voluntary initiative to help defend companies against criticism by demonstrating their good practices more publicly and transparently. The case studies in this chapter highlight some examples of some of the things that large corporations have begun to do to incorporate better responsibility and sustainability practices, but it must be noted that, despite their best efforts, each one of them still has significant sustainability and responsibility issues to deal with, simply because of the nature of the business in which the company operates.[11]

On the darker side, many corporations, especially in the US and China, are linked to governments through their political action committees, lobbying activities and ownership structures. Sometimes these contributions and lobbyists' efforts are in direct contradiction to activities that companies are undertaking on the social or sustainability side, and for which they are claiming credit publicly, while the lobbying activities are often much less transparent. Corporate political activities typically serve the company's profit-maximising orientation, sometimes at the expense of society or the environment. Contradictions can happen; for instance, when companies lobby against taxes that governments could use to help alleviate poverty while simultaneously instituting poverty reduction programmes. Further, too many companies still use hazardous materials to produce their goods, or have problems in their supply and distribution networks, or have manufacturing operations with poor labour or environmental standards. Others produce products that are of questionable value, employing high pressure marketing tactics to sell ever more goods and services to a public that, as debt levels prior to the economic collapse of 2008 suggested, was already overspent.

11 These examples were developed with the research assistance of Samantha Cereceda, MBA, Boston College.

Box 2 **BT (British Telecom)**

As part of the telecommunications industry that customers love to hate, BT's CSR strategy is to grow its business profitably and sustainably by providing services and products that benefit its customers, society and the environment.[12] According to the company, its major initiatives include: helping to tackle climate change, working with employees and suppliers to reduce energy consumption, developing sustainable customer solutions, meeting growing demand for lower-carbon products and services, enabling skills for an inclusive society, and playing a part in creating a connected world where everyone benefits from technology.[13] These goals are supplemented by: a focus on reducing the company's carbon footprint; continual improvement of environmental performance; creating profitable products and services that benefit people, economies and the environment; and working with community partners to increase communication skills. The company claims to be committed to ethical business through its 'Way We Work' code of conduct and statement of business practice, 'getting it right' for customers, supporting its people and communities, and ensuring that its suppliers adopt high standards on issues such as product stewardship.

As noted in its *Sustainability Report* 2010, BT assesses its performance on numerous indicators, including minimising service disruption after a disaster, accessibility of products to people of all ages and abilities, environmental impacts of business travel, consumer privacy, data protection and customer satisfaction. It seeks to promote the use of communications technology to help work-life balance, energy use, climate change impacts and carbon reporting, among others. One of the more important things that BT does is to embed performance on these issues into key performance indicators (KPIs) on which it assesses overall performance. Among its KPIs are: business integrity; waste to landfill; carbon dioxide emissions; customer service; employee engagement; diversity performance; lost-time injury rates; absenteeism; supplier relations; and ethical trading. The company also measures performance against what it calls 'improving society' through a minimum investment of 1% of pre-tax profits in community programmes, which are independently evaluated.

---

12 www.btplc.com/Responsiblebusiness/Ourstory/Sustainabilityreport/index.aspx.
13 BT website, corporate responsibility strategy, www.btplc.com/
   Responsiblebusiness/Ourstory/Sustainabilityreport/section/index.
   aspx?sectionid=b473c594-c302-453b-9c68-5167b84b7920, accessed 22 December
   2010.

Redesigning the corporation for tomorrow's needs

There appear to be significant limits on how far corporate responsibility and sustainability measures, particularly voluntary measures, can (or even should) be taken. These limits are especially notable when the corporation is accepted in its current form, in part because of the generally accepted 'wisdom' that the sole purpose of the firm is to maximise shareholder wealth. This notion derives from the thinking of neoclassical economics, whose main spokesperson was the late Milton Friedman. In the US, the *Dodge v. Ford* ruling[14] gave this perspective a legal underpinning. However, legal scholar Lynn Stout argues (2008: 176):

> Corporations are purely legal creatures, without flesh, blood or bone. Their existence and behaviour is determined by a web of legal rules found in corporate charters and bylaws, private contracts, and a host of federal and state regulations . . . This is why lawyers, and especially law professors, should resist the siren song of *Dodge v. Ford* [the legal case that, purportedly but erroneously, established the wealth maximisation norm]. We are not in the business of imparting fables, however charming. We are in the business of instructing clients and students in the realities of the corporate form. Corporations seek profits for shareholders, but they seek other things as well, including specific investment, stakeholder benefits, and their own continued existing. Teaching *Dodge v. Ford* as anything but an example of judicial mistake obstructs understanding of this reality.

Further, as we shall see in later chapters, technological advances, ecological and social constraints, and a desire for new types of enterprise and opportunities have created a context in which a wide variety of adaptations are beginning to evolve. One initiative underway in the US focuses explicitly on the way that corporations are designed, arguing that the current design, which is a product of the 19th century, is not suited to the world that companies face today.

Corporation 2020, a multi-sector collaborative initiative, aims to redesign the corporation to better meet the needs of the 21st century. Corporation 2020 seeks to design a corporate form that 'seamlessly integrate[s] both social and financial purpose'. A core premise of Corporation 2020 is that society's expectations of business are changing dramatically—and

---

14   204 Mich. 459, 170 N.W. 668. (Mich. 1919).

that companies will increasingly be expected to make constructive and positive contributions towards solving serious social, economic and ecological global problems. Corporation 2020 represents a step beyond traditional approaches to CSR, asking: 'How do we design corporations such that their core purpose is to harness the resources of private interests in service to the public interest?'

Corporation 2020 proposes six 'principles of corporate design'. At the core of the principles is a redefinition of corporate purpose, in effect, returning the corporation to its original roots of serving the public interest (Greenfield 2005). Another key element is to shift the focus of corporations away from a narrow conception of who is to be served towards a broader concept; that is, away from shareholder primacy toward stakeholder primacy. The six principles are:[15]

- The purpose of the corporation is to harness private interests to serve the public interest;

- Corporations shall accrue fair returns for shareholders, but not at the expense of the legitimate interests of other stakeholders;

- Corporations shall operate sustainably, meeting the needs of the present generation without compromising the ability of future generations to meet their needs;

- Corporations shall distribute their wealth equitably among those who contribute to its creation;

- Corporations shall be governed in a manner that is participatory, transparent, ethical and accountable;

- Corporations shall not infringe on the right of natural persons to govern themselves, nor infringe on other universal human rights.

Importantly, the concept at the core of Corporation 2020's principles is not 'maximised' returns but, rather, fair returns—to all of those who have legitimately invested in the firm, not just shareholders. This orientation recognises that it is not just shareholders who invest resources, other stakeholders do so as well. For example, customers invest their trust and their franchise in the firm when purchasing products and services. Employees invest their intellectual capital (and sometimes their physical capabilities as well), as well as their loyalty and commitment. Suppliers

15 www.corporation2020.org, accessed 28 April 2009.

and distributors may well invest in company-specific infrastructure (as noted in the discussion above on the extended enterprise) to better meet their customer's needs. Even secondary stakeholders make investments in companies. For example, communities may invest in infrastructure that specifically helps companies (Waddock 2009)

A related, but longer-standing, initiative in the UK is Tomorrow's Company,[16] a research and education initiative that builds bridges between companies and business leaders, helping businesses develop and implement progressive ideas to pursue a sustainable future. By undertaking cutting-edge research on issues such business leadership, corporate reporting and corporate responsibility, Tomorrow's Company helps set the agenda for progressive businesses in the UK. Early on, Tomorrow's Company recognised the need to develop leadership talent that could operate effectively in what it calls the 'triple context' of business, ecosystems and communities. It has also focused on stewardship of resources, raising early and critical questions about the growing discrepancy between the financial and real economies in what it terms the 'global casino economy'.

Tomorrow's Company argues for a changed mindset among business leaders. In particular, it believes that 'global companies can be a force for good and are uniquely placed to deliver the practical solutions that are urgently required to address these issues'. Changing mindsets will require:[17]

- A redefinition of success so that it aligns and integrates social, ecological, human and financial aspects;

- Embedding and communicating values into companies so they can be defined and assessed by their alignment with those values;

- Creating sound national regulatory frameworks and international agreements that support these objectives, and working across governmental and NGO boundaries in the development process.

One of the current issues making any transition toward these objectives difficult is the notion of corporate personhood as discussed in the next section.

---

16 www.tomorrowscompany.com.
17 'Tomorrow's Global Company: Challenges and Choices, Executive Summary', www.tomorrowscompany.com/uploads/TGCexcu.pdf, accessed 28 January 2010.

Box 3 **Coca-Cola**

The Coca-Cola Company, which in recent years has taken many positive steps to deal with issues of sustainability, is a leading member of the soft drink beverage industry and also has significant interests in the bottled water industry. Whilst the company is taking steps to deal with some of the issues posed by its business model, which promotes sugary drinks with high calories and bottled water with both resource-use and disposal issues, it nevertheless faces criticism for its role in the developed world's obesity crisis, and around issues of waste and of water usage associated with bottled water. Coca-Cola's goals and targets on sustainability are divided into: active healthy living; energy management and climate protection; community; sustainable packaging; and water stewardship.[18] Its sustainability platform 'Live Positively' commits the company 'to make a positive difference in the world by redesigning the way we work and live so sustainability is part of everything we do'.[19] Here, we focus on the healthy living and water use components of Coca-Cola's sustainability strategy.

Coca-Cola has developed specific goals with respect to each of its goals. For example, with respect to water stewardship, the company aims to 'improve water efficiency by 20% by 2012, compared with a 2004 baseline, to return to the environment, at a level that supports aquatic life, the water we use in our system operations by the end of 2010 through comprehensive wastewater treatment'.[20]

A second goal focuses on a healthy living programme that started in 2006 at a cost of US$3 million, rising to US$9 million in 2009. The company states: 'We aspire to help people around the world lead active healthy lives through the variety and availability of the beverages we produce; our assortment of package sizes; the ingredients, nutrition and health information we provide; our responsible marketing practices; and our support for physical activity programmes. We provide product and package variety across our markets. We have more than 750 low-and no-calorie beverages in our portfolio, and we continue to introduce new low-and no-calorie options, as well as nutritionally fortified products, each year.'

Obviously, the company faces a conundrum around 'healthy living' when so many of its products are high-sugar, high-calorie, low-nutritional-

---

18 Coca-Cola, '2008/2009 Sustainability Review', www.thecoca-colacompany.com/citizenship/pdf/2008-2009_sustainability_review.pdf, accessed 17 December 2009.

19 www.thecoca-colacompany.com/citizenship/index.html.

20 'Environmental Water Stewardship', www.thecoca-colacompany.com/citizenship/water_main.html, accessed 20 December 2009.

value products. Coca-Cola claims to provide education (to help people make healthy choices in their lives), variety (of beverages and packages to consumers) and physical activity (through encouragement, sponsorship and grassroots programmes).[21] Campaigns by other entities (such as a YouTube video issued by the City of New York),[22] however, have been trying to influence consumers not to drink sugary beverages at all. The American Beverage Association (ABA)[23] counterclaimed that 'since 1998, calories in for-sale beverages have declined by 21%'. It is the ABA that generally responds to such campaigns through its news releases and statements, rather than the companies themselves. Coca-Cola (as well as Pepsi and Dr Pepper, among others) are members of the ABA. The ABA joined a US$9 million lobbying campaign to avert a threatened US government tax on sugary drinks. In May 2006, the beverage industry developed national school beverage guidelines with the Alliance for a Healthier Generation, a joint initiative by the William J. Clinton Foundation and the American Heart Association. The industry committed to changing the beverage mix in schools across America by removing full-calorie soft drinks, as well as capping calories and reducing portion sizes on other beverages, and providing nutritious beverage options by the beginning of the 2009–2010 school year.

Consumers are also keeping a close eye on Coca-Cola. In October 2009, Coca-Cola teamed up with the American Academy of Family Physicians to form the Consumer Alliance Programme to help consumers make better choices with regard to beverages and artificial sweeteners.[24] Coca-Cola provided a grant of US$500,000. The news caused outrage, with a number of AAFP members resigning in protest.[25] Despite the protests, as a result of attempting to deal proactively with these issues, Coca-Cola holds the 36th spot in the Newsweek's Green Rankings, while it is in the first place in the food and beverage category.[26] In 2009, Coca-Cola made it onto the Dow Jones Sustainability World Index and has consistently appeared in

21 'Healthy Living—Active Living', www.thecoca-colacompany.com/citizenship/ fitness_active_lifestyles.html, accessed 18 December 2009.

22 www.youtube.com/user/DrinkingFat.

23 www.ameribev.org.

24 American Academy of Family Physicians, 'Coca-Cola Grant Launches AAFP Consumer Alliance Programme', News Release, www.aafp.org/online/en/home/ publications/news/news-now/inside-aafp/20091006cons-alli-coke.html, accessed 17 December 2009.

25 'Outrage Over Coca-Cola and AAFP Team Up', www.twirlit.com/2009/11/24/ outrage-over-coca-cola-and-aafp-team-up, accessed 17 December 2009.

26 greenrankings.newsweek.com/companies/industry/food-and-beverage, accessed 17 December 2009.

the Dow Jones North America Index and the FTSE4Good Index. In 2009 it also received the 'Green Choice Award' from *Natural Health Magazine*.

Corporate personhood

In January 2010 the US Supreme Court issued a stunning decision in the Citizens United case that overturned decades of laws and limitations on corporate speech and participation in the democratic process by throwing out restrictions on corporate contributions to political campaigns and effectively giving corporations the same free speech rights as individuals. The controversial decision led many to believe that US democracy was itself at risk because of the potential corrupting influence of money on campaigns and, ultimately, on legislation. A growing movement to end corporate 'personhood' has been revitalised.[27] Claiming that to limit corporate 'speech' and campaign contributions constituted a violation of the US Constitution, the slim majority of justices (in a 5–4 decision) argued that the public deserved to hear points of view from many parties, including corporations, and that government should not be in the business of limiting 'free speech'.

The decision followed years of attempting to limit corporate influence over politics in the US, which legal scholar Lawrence Lessig claims creates the type of institutional corruption noted above. Fearing the worst of this institutional corruption in politics, US President Barack Obama noted that the decision would result in 'a stampede of special interest money in our politics'. The decision brought the issue of corporate 'personhood' into public prominence in the US, highlighting years of less public controversy about whether corporations should be treated as persons in the law. Corporate 'personhood', according to the activist group Reclaim Democracy, is a 'claim that corporations were intended to fully enjoy the legal status and protections created for human beings',[28] despite the reality that they are not human (although populated with humans). Writing in the *Boston Globe*, legal scholar Kent Greenfield (2010a) observed:

27 For background see, for example, *New York Times* 2009b and Liptak 2010.
28 Reclaim Democracy, 'Introduction to Corporate Personhood', www.reclaimdemocracy.org/personhood, accessed 28 January 2010.

The fundamental problem with Justice Anthony Kennedy's majority opinion is not his view of the First Amendment. Rather, it is his misguided view of the nature of corporations. To Kennedy, there is no difference between humans and corporations for purposes of the free speech analysis. But he forgets that corporations are not natural beings—they are artificial institutions. When people start businesses, states award them corporate charters as a kind of public subsidy. The corporate form provides the protection of limited liability, protecting shareholders from personal liability for debts of the company. The charter also bestows the corporation with a legal 'personality' separate from its investors, so that it can sue and be sued without the participation of each shareholder. What's more, charters also give corporations an unlimited life span, allowing them to outlast their founders.

The fear, according to Greenfield, is that, 'in the name of free speech—the speech of those of us who are real, breathing humans will be drowned out by the blather of Walmart, Goldman Sachs, ExxonMobil and other for-profit corporations' (Greenfield 2010b). Although that fear had existed for many years, limitations on corporate spending in politics had at least had the semblance of reducing the institutional corruption that Lessig identified, and to some extent attempting to put limits on corporate power.

The fundamental problem of corporate personhood has to do with the accepted definition that corporations exist to 'maximise shareholder wealth', rather than (as in the earliest days of corporations) to serve the public interest. In this profit maximisation process too many corporations externalise costs where they can in the interest of efficiency. They view these externalities not through the societal or ecological lens, but solely through the corporate lens. But the reality is that externalised costs remain in society or nature—and someone has to pay somehow, whether through taxes, reduced wellbeing, or other types of 'payment'.

It is difficult to make massive cultural shifts within large organisations, be they corporations or other institutions. Also, as we noted earlier, the CR banner has been taken up largely by highly visible, branded or very progressive firms, with visionary leadership. Thus, many large companies are likely to continue with business-as-usual until the regulatory, legal and societal contexts force them to change. But emerging alongside modern corporations and multinational firms are new types of enterprise (some for-profit and others not) that constitute the heart of the emerging SEE Change, which we will discuss in the next chapters. One theory of how change in the economy towards a more sustainable enterprise economy will occur, then, is that it will come not from existing entities, but rather from start-ups and newer forms that are created with a very different purpose and mindset than the traditional corporation, however progressive it might be.

Box 4 **Dell**

In 2009, computer giant Dell took the first place in the inaugural Corporate Sustainability Index, a survey of technology firms' sustainability efforts put together by Technology Business Research,[29] ahead of Hewlett-Packard, BT or Intel. Although in 2009, in the first-ever *Newsweek* Green rankings Dell was placed second to Hewlett-Packard overall (not just in the technology sector), it was placed first overall in 2010.[30] Among other things, Dell offers free computer recycling to consumers worldwide and sources 35% of its US energy from green power. According to *Environmental Leader*: 'Dell, which comes in at number two, ranks fourth among the top US corporate users of renewable energy, and leads the industry with its product take-back and recycling programmes. Its headquarters uses 100% renewable energy and all its desktop and laptop computers will consume up to 25% less energy by 2010 . . . Dell became carbon neutral in 2008 by using offsets and other methods, and plans to maintain its carbon neutrality for the next five years.'[31]

Other areas that Dell emphasises through its corporate accountability are its standards, ethics and compliance, supplier responsibility, finance, governance and management, regulatory compliance and stakeholder engagement. In the area of CR, Dell's 2010 goals include: increasing communications about CR to customers, stakeholder and employees; adding dynamic online links to dell.com within the summary report; and advancing its strategy to become the greenest technology company on the planet through its Enviro 2.0 business platform. In addition, Dell plans to increase its take-back of waste equipment to one billion pounds (approx. 453 million kg) and reduce operational greenhouse gas emissions by 15% by 2010, committing to a carbon-neutral operation for five years, with a goal of 40% reduction by 2015.[32] And these are only a few of the specific goals that Dell has advanced along sustainability and CR dimensions.

---

29 en.community.dell.com/dell-blogs/enterprise/b/inside-enterprise-it/archive/2009/02/20/dell-takes-no-1-spot-in-tbr-customer-satisfaction-survey-for-servers.aspx, accessed 12 March 2011.

30 *Newsweek*, 'Green Rankings 2009', greenrankings.newsweek.com/top500, accessed 29 January 2010; *Newsweek*, 'Green Rankings 2010', www.newsweek.com/2010/10/18/green-rankings-us-companies.html, accessed 22 December 2010.

31 'HP, Dell, J&J, Intel and IBM Top Newsweek's Inaugural Green Rankings', Environmental Leader, www.environmentalleader.com/2009/09/22/hp-dell-jj-intel-and-ibm-top-newsweeks-inaugural-green-rankings, accessed 17 December 2009.

32 content.dell.com/us/en/corp/d/corp-comm/kpi.aspx.

Box 5 **Dupont**

Another company that has moved significantly towards sustainability (along with its counterpart Dow Chemicals) is Dupont, one of the leaders in the chemical industry. Dupont chair, Charles Holliday, co-authored the book *Walking the Talk: The Business Case for Sustainable Development* with Shell's and Anova's CEOs. According to Holliday, Dupont is focusing on sustainable growth, which he defines as 'creating shareholder and societal value while reducing the environmental footprint along our value lines' (Holliday *et al.* 2002). Even though some of the company's products are inevitably hazardous simply by virtue of its being a chemical company, most are designed to enhance life and work. Dupont, like others in its sector, emphasises sustainability through long-term goals (taken out to 2015 as of 2010), including reducing greenhouse gas emissions by 15% beyond the 72% already achieved, reducing global water consumption by 30% over ten years and offsetting increased production volumes through conservation, reuse and recycling. Further, DuPont, has already reduced global atmospheric carcinogen emissions by 92% and aims at a further reduction of 50% from the base year of 2004 by 2015, bringing total reductions since 1990 down a staggering 96%. The company has similar stringent goals for fleet fuel efficiency, and aims to have all its sustainability practices independently audited by 2015.[33]

33 '2015 Sustainability Goals: DuPont Footprint', www2.dupont.com/Sustainability/en_US/Footprint/index.html, accessed 20 December 2009.

Box 6 **Mitsubishi**

A member of the 100 Most Sustainable Companies[34] is Japan's Mitsubishi which, in 2008, appointed its CEO, Ryoichi Ueda, as its chief sustainability officer; the company was already investing heavily in reducing carbon dioxide emissions by 30% and installing solar power generators. The company is Japan's largest general trading concern, consisting of some 500 member companies at 200 locations in around 80 countries. It is involved in many industries, including energy, metals, machinery, chemicals, food and general merchandise. The company's stated goal is 'to contribute to the enrichment of society through business firmly rooted in principles of fairness and integrity'.[35] Mitsubishi's sustainability initiatives operate within three corporate principles: corporate responsibility to society (*shoki hoko*) — striving to enrich society, both materially and spiritually, while contributing towards the preservation of the global environment; integrity and fairness (*shoji komei*) — maintaining principles of transparency and openness, conducting business with integrity and fairness; and international understanding through trade (*ritsugyo boeki*) — expanding business based on an all-encompassing global perspective.[36] Further, the company emphasises respect for human rights, environmental management and stakeholder relationships through a management system that reports directly to the executive committee on these matters.[37]

34 www.global100.org
35 www.mitsubishicorp.com/jp/en/about/mc, accessed 29 January 2010.
36 www.mitsubishicorp.com/jp/en/csr/library/sr2009/feature1/principles.html, accessed 29 January 2010.
37 Many more details can be found at www.mitsubishicorp.com/jp/en/csr/vision, accessed 29 January 2010.

5
Business Unusual 2.0

In the last chapter, we explored how big businesses are beginning to deal with issues of sustainability and responsibility, and how they need to continue to change to meet the emerging demands of a sustainable enterprise economy. As we noted, that change will not be easy for them, as large-scale change is difficult at best, and sometimes can be next to impossible. But things do change, and in our world the pace of change seems incredible at times—socially, economically and in other domains. Since 1995 when the World Wide Web blossomed into public awareness, and graphical interfaces became useful tools for the general public, electronic connectivity in all its various forms has reshaped how humans, especially in developed nations, but increasingly in developing nations as well, relate to the world.

The economist Joseph Schumpeter argued that economies were never actually stable because change was always underway. In Schumpeter's view, change through what he called 'creative destruction' would occur by necessity because of the 'fundamental impulse' that 'comes from the new consumers, goods, the new methods of production or transportation, the new markets, the new forms of industrial organisation that capitalist enterprise creates' (Schumpeter 1962: 82) Noting that this process of creative destruction was the 'essential fact about capitalism', Schumpeter pointed out that creative destruction comes, not from outside the system, but actually from within. Indeed, he argued that this form of creativity was a product of the very entrepreneurial process that underpins the whole notion of capitalism (Schumpeter 1962: 82-84).

Today, we see this same process of creative destruction occurring through what we are calling SEE Change, because entrepreneurs are building new types of enterprises, some based on the emerging 'cloud' of web-connectivity, others based on a multiple-bottom-line set of purposes from their inception. Still others, as we will explore in Chapter 6, span traditional boundaries to find new solutions to what management theorist Russell Ackoff (1975) once called 'messes' and what others have called 'wicked problems' (Churchman 1967). Messes are problems too complex to be solved by one organisation, or even organisations within one sector, because they inherently cross boundaries. Wicked problems are, 'that class of social system problems which are ill-formulated, where the information is confusing, where there are many clients and decision-makers with conflicting values, and where the ramifications in the whole system are thoroughly confusing' (Churchman 1967: B141).

In many respects, the whole movement towards a sustainable enterprise economy tackles one of these wicked problems, simply because moving in this direction necessitates that multiple considerations be built into enterprises of all sorts. Such enterprises go well beyond the simple single bottom-line of maximising shareholder wealth because many stakeholders' interests need to be taken into consideration, and because the problems of society and the environment are difficult to resolve by any other means. Below we will explore some characteristics, and give a few brief examples, of these emerging SEE Change enterprises.

Enterprises of the cloud

Increasingly, as new enterprises evolve, we witness the intersection of multiple affective local communities in and near our homes, in our public spaces and in private places. Many of the affective communities to which we belong are in the ethos of what some call the 'cloud'—the interlinked web of computers with no particular location but which feels local. Enterprises of the cloud link us in sometimes intimate ways to others sharing common interests in cyberspace, as well as to businesses that we can interact with online. Companies such as Amazon, eBay and Google have capitalised on the cloud concept for their business models.

Social media and the cloud

The affective communities created by social media within the cloud create a sense of belonging, even though participants may never meet in person. For example, entities such as MySpace, Facebook and eBay create a sense of membership and shared participation by connecting people in various ways. Facebook and MySpace serve the direct purpose of connecting people in networks and keeping those in the networks informed about the activities of others. EBay uses cloud computing technologies to sell items to a wide range of customers, linking seller and customer, and using customer ratings to engender trust between the two.

Through these web-based entities, and many others like them, we participate in a cloud of information resources and connectivity. We also increasingly share our secrets either directly by revealing them or because our web-based movements—our every click, our every purchase—are monitored. Indeed, in many parts of the world, webcams (web-based cameras connected to computers) seem ubiquitous, making our physical movements, as well as our web-based ones, potentially public.

In addition to emerging forms of enterprise that are relatively more permanent, there are numerous other types of organised activities, some quite short-lived, that rely on cloud computing technologies. For example, flash mobs and smart mobs rely on technological connections through blogs, MySpace, Facebook, Twitter and other Web 2.0 connectivity formats still rapidly evolving. 'Smart mobs', according to Howard Rheingold (2002), who invented the term, are short-term self-organised systems, structures or entities that form for a brief period through the use of electronic technologies such as cell phones, personal digital assistants and peer-to-peer networks, then dissolve. Rheingold wrote about smart mobs in 2002, pointing out that new wireless electronic devices enable people who do not know each other to act together purposefully—both for positive and sometimes not so positive purposes. EBay's quality control system, in which users rate the credibility and quality of sellers, is a form of smart mob. Other types are formed to organise protests or responses to a political situation, as happened largely via email in Seattle for the 1999 protests against the WTO.

Flash mobs are even more temporary than smart mobs, as they are groups that form to do something, then dissipate just as quickly. Apparently spontaneous (but having been organised ahead usually via web-based connectivity), flash mobs sing, dance, stop moving for a period of time, act or perform in some other way that attracts public attention.

Sometimes their antics are recorded and appear on social media such as YouTube. Some are for good causes, others just for fun.

Peer-to-peer resource sharing via the Internet is a use of electronic technology that is threatening traditional media companies. For example, despite the crackdown on Napster (which originally allowed free downloads of music), other peer-to-peer sharing technologies have emerged that permit music, film and television programming downloads (e.g. Hulu, BitTorrent, Limewire, Shareaza, Kazaa and a multitude of others). These new media make traditional industry approaches, which attempt to control content and distribution as well as profits, problematic in the future at best. Proponents claim that peer-to-peer networks and sharing creates greater democracy and access to resources, while the producers of some of those resources (e.g. media companies) claim that their intellectual or artistic capital resources are being stolen. Other applications are forming new business models (e.g. Skype, the free internet phone service).

Peer-to-peer technologies also inform other applications; for example, 'freeware', software developed voluntarily by contributors for numerous types of applications. One such application of freeware is an open-sourced version of Microsoft Office that competes directly with the software giant. Another is the web-based encyclopaedia Wikipedia, to which anyone can contribute (or edit and add to already submitted items), and which is accessible to all at no cost, providing significant competition to traditional encyclopaedia publishers who find it hard to compete effectively with the instant-access, constantly updated 'wiki' form.[1]

Traditional newspapers and magazines are also threatened by the new social media, notably blogs and other forms of web logging. The word 'blog' is a contraction of the term 'web log'. It is a website to which a person, group or organisation contributes ideas, images and other information on a regular or periodic basis. Some blogs provide constantly updated communications about events, news, gossip and just about anything else one might think of. One of the more famous blogs in the US is the Huffington Post. Blogs now exist on topics from politics to food to books, and are as formalised as the Huffington Post or as simple as an individual writing about his or her own ideas and opinions. By some estimates, there are as many as 200 million blogs in the world, about 73 million of them in China (Appleyard 2009).

---

1 A 'wiki' is a website that allows people to collaborate on a central document, project or idea development from local computers.

The SmartMob blog points out that on-the-spot citizens can react more quickly than traditional media to spread the word, but 'blogs are opinion; journalism is fact'. Most people can't tell the difference.' However, fact checking, analysis and in-depth reporting still probably have a place in the world.[2] As SmartMob's creator Howard Rheingold points out:[3]

> So you are seeing the recording industry and the motion picture industry with digital rights management; you are seeing the extension of copyrights by the big companies that are copyright holders, and who are actually taking-in the control of the use of technology in what they call 'trusted computing.'

Social media, and the emerging types of enterprises based on them, have the capacity to connect us to each other in wholly new (and sometimes frightening) ways. They also provide access to a wealth of information that exists nowhere and everywhere in that ineffable cloud of networked computers that we call cyberspace, particularly the Web 2.0 version of cyberspace. The electronic devices that support them connect us to others on a, not always positive, 24/7 basis, changing the nature of what privacy means.

In addition, blogs (along with other social media) can put enterprises of all sorts—large and small businesses, as well as NGOs, CSOs and governments—into the spotlight quickly and widely, depending on their reach. In doing so, they create significantly greater transparency for enterprises—sometimes more than those enterprises might wish. The sustainable enterprise economy, which is arising in part out of these new media, thus inherently carries with it greater degrees of transparency than were available in the past. Combined with this virtual transparency is a degree of 'dematerialisation' that comes with electronic technologies and is an essential part of SEE Change.

2 SmartMobs, 'Blogging Good or Bad for Journalism?' www.smartmobs. com/2010/01/31/blogging-helps-to-make-the-news-a-bit-more-personal/?utm_source=feedburner&utm_medium=feed&utm_campaign=Feed%3A+SmartMobs+%28Smart+Mobs%29, accessed 2 February 2010.

3 Robin Good, 'Web 2.0 Meets SmartMobs: Howard Rheingold's Views on Web 2.0', 4 October 2006, www.masternewmedia.org/news/2006/10/04/web_20_meets_smartmobs_howard.htm, accessed 2 February 2010.

Dematerialisation, servicisation and enterprise

As Schumpeter's theory of creative destruction proposes, the changes that have already taken place to provide new enterprises in our economy today have come from what were once small start-ups that have grown rapidly to have major impacts on individuals, and have even changed society in significant ways. Electronic connectivity makes getting and using information far easier than it used to be. Many of these new types of companies are 'dematerialising' the economy, at least to some extent, through digital technologies or through initiatives known as 'servicising'.

Dematerialisation

Here is a brief thought experiment that may help provide insight into the processes of dematerialisation created by the electronic infrastructure. Think of going to a library and ploughing through volumes of books on long shelves filled with other books, along with the physical infrastructure and resources required to produce and house those books over time. Compare that to searching the Internet for the same information. Not only is the search considerably less time consuming, but it is also less physically resource intensive, since you can access many information resources without necessarily needing hard copies.

Consider the dominant presence of Google as a search engine. Think about the ways in which social networking media, such as Facebook, MySpace, YouTube, LinkedIn and Ning, allow people to put information about themselves online, communicate with many others or organise events. Consider that starting from almost nothing in 2005, YouTube now hosts millions of publicly available videos (one estimate in 2008 put the number at 140 million[4]), with about 1.2 billion downloads daily in 2009,[5] and is currently the leading online video source. And much of this viewing, uploading and downloading takes place electronically rather than through DVDs, videos or other physical formats.

---

4 beerpla.net/2008/08/14/how-to-find-out-the-number-of-videos-on-youtube.
5 Michael Arrington, 'YouTube Video Streams Top 1.2 Billion/Day', Tech Crunch, 9 June 2009, www.techcrunch.com/2009/06/09/youtube-video-streams-top-1-billionday, accessed 2 February 2010.

Think of how, instead of going to a shop to buy music CDs, many people now download music directly to their computer, phone, MP3 player, iPod or other device. There is no tangible physical material in the 'production process' of obtaining the music other than the device and its connectivity. Indeed, some analysts predict that soon the CD will go the way of eight-track tapes and record albums—into the dustbin of memory. Or think about how Amazon's Kindle, other e-books and Apple's iPad are transforming the book-selling, news, magazine and publishing industry in general, moving these formerly physical products into digital formats rather more quickly than many traditional publishers might wish. The same is true of DVDs and videos as 'on demand' services such as TiVo and other technologies change how we relate to visual forms. Or think about how emailing, texting, Twittering, Skyping, network-based conferencing and other forms of instant communication have changed people's availability and, ultimately, their lives, as well as reducing the need for printed communications and, sometimes, for travel.

One example is telling. Since the late 1990s, many companies have begun producing multiple-bottom-line reports of various sorts (social reports, environmental reports, sustainability reports, triple-bottom-line reports, etc.). Initially, many companies used reams of paper, ink and graphical supplies to produce these reports, distributing them widely. While most companies still do produce some physical copies of their multiple-bottom-line reports, many produce far fewer than they originally believed necessary. In fact, they realise that users have specific interests and actually may prefer to access specific parts of the report online, either on the company's website or in pdf format that they can download to their own computers. The need for printed copies is drastically reduced and dissemination can be focused on the particular needs and interests of potential users.

Activists, critics, NGOs and interest groups now organise themselves electronically and/or online without needing to put up a single poster or hand out a single leaflet. Companies can do much the same thing with their marketing. Political elections, as Barack Obama's 2009 presidential campaign demonstrated, now depend as much on electronic connectivity as on traditional paper-based approaches for fund-raising, consciousness-raising and political action.

'Info-mediaries' are web-based collectors of information that essentially serve as neutral intermediaries between those entities with information or something to sell and those who want that information or to make a purchase (Hagel and Rayport 1997). By such means, you can find long-lost friends and relatives, look up addresses and telephone numbers, and buy just about anything your heart desires. All of this is not to mention the relative ease of finding information through online resources. Companies such as eBay, Amazon and PayPal have changed how consumers in developed nations think about buying goods and services, and shifted the momentum of growth in their direction. And this has all happened very recently—before 1995 none of it was feasible.

Interestingly, all of these applications take what used to be material-intensive applications (e.g. paper, ink, plastics and other material resources) and provide the same service or product but without the direct materials costs. Of course there are many (and problematic) resource issues associated with producing the electricity needed for electronic communications, as well as dealing with electronic waste which is now at monumental proportions. But the dematerialisation that has taken place already has the potential to significantly shift resource usage.

E-waste

The downside of all of this digitalisation is that many raw materials are needed to produce electronic gadgets, some of them quite hazardous or rare. In addition, because software and devices change so rapidly, many of these devices are (often deliberately) designed to be outdated within a few months of purchase. Producers are quite willing to keep changing electronic devices so that they become obsolete quickly, forcing customers to purchase newer versions even when the old ones are still working well.

Electronic waste has become a huge environmental issue. The US Environmental Protection Agency estimates that in 2007 the US alone disposed of 26.9 million televisions, 205.5 million computer products and 140.3 million mobile phones. Of these, only 18% of televisions and computer products, and 10% of mobile phones were recycled. It is estimated that, globally, between 20 million and 590 million tonnes of e-waste are generated annually, with projections for a 3–5% annual increase (US EPA 2008: 23).

The Electronics Takeback Coalition points out that not only is e-waste difficult to recycle, but e-equipment quickly becomes obsolete, contains numerous hazardous compounds and most ends up in landfills. Even when people believe they are recycling their old equipment, as much as 50% to 80% of that e-waste is actually shipped to developing countries. There it is dismantled by workers working in very poor conditions, handling toxic materials such as lead, cadmium and mercury, and frequently without adequate health and safety measures in place. The problem is compounded by the rapid pace of equipment replacement (e.g. it is estimated that, globally, as many as 419 million computers will be sold every year by 2013). Sales figures for mobile phones are even higher, estimated at 1.18 billion in 2008, and estimates put the number of mobile phone subscribers at four billion worldwide.[6] Thus, for all the dematerialisation associated with digitalisation processes, there are clearly side-effects around resource usage that need to be dealt with.

Servicisation

Another notable trend, at least in some product categories and industries, is the movement towards a product-service system (Mont 2002), also known as servicisation (White, Stoughton and Feng 1999). According to Mont (2002: 237), the frequently unrecognised imperative is that population pressures and increased consumption levels will mean that, by the middle of the 21st century, resource productivity may well need to increase ten-fold. Servicising represents an emerging form of dematerialisation in which customers get the same level of performance from products and services but with a reduced environmental burden through improved utility or usefulness. The concept is based on functionality, or what ecologist Amory Lovins has observed: 'People don't want heating fuel or coolant; people want cold beer and hot showers.'[6]

The idea of servicisation is gaining traction because in developed countries some 70% of the economy is now service- rather than production-based. Facing the reality of ecological stresses and limits, companies moving into servicising are shifting the boundaries between manufacturing and production, and services. The notion of product-service systems is 'a marketable set of products and services capable of jointly fulfilling a user's need' (Mont 2002: 238). In this context, servicisation means that a company upgrades a customer's product by providing more services, for example by leasing the use of the product rather than selling the actual product, creating an orientation toward repairing rather than replacing products, and changing customer attitudes from product sales to receiving services that help to upgrade the product (Mont 2002: 238-39).

With servicising, the company sells the functionality of a product to a user, upgrading as necessary, rather than necessarily selling the product

6 www.business.gov/expand/green-business/product-development/servicizing. html, accessed 4 February 2010.

itself. These approaches, and others, are evolving to help reduce consumption by focusing the customer on intangible or non-material goods or improvements from service, rather than on simply purchasing a new product. Servicising means that the product is not actually 'sold' in the traditional sense to customers, but is rather leased or rented. The producer then becomes more responsible for the full life-cycle costs of its product. Furthermore, when a product is shared among users, less material resources are needed. Some areas where product-service systems or servicisation appeals are chemicals management (e.g. the customer buys cleaning services rather than cleaning products), transportation services (see the Zipcar example below) and furnishings (the customer rents rather than purchases furnishings) (White, Stoughton and Feng 1999).

Some companies have begun to pick up on the notion of servicisation. For example, in some US cities, individuals can rent a Zipcar or, in the Netherlands, can contact Call-a-Car. These services provide a car shared among many users, for short periods of time and only when they actually need a car, allowing customers to rent the service of transportation rather than purchasing and owning their own vehicle with all the associated expenses and material costs to the natural environment. Another well known example is that of the carpet manufacturer Interface which leases squares of recyclable carpet to customers and replaces only the worn squares. Apple's iTunes application represents another form of servicising, as Apple is selling a licence to listen to the music rather than a physical product such as a CD. A further example is the Xerox Corporation which, during the 1990s, transformed itself from a copier manufacturer into a documents management service that helps customers reduce the overall number of devices in their offices while simultaneously selling more of the company's products and services via equipment consolidation (Rothenberg 2007).

Enterprise Unusual

The for-benefit corporation, B corporation and conscious capitalism

Dematerialisation and servicising, along with the CR and sustainability initiatives discussed in the last chapter, are only some of the moves towards SEE Change. In addition, as this section will discuss, there are many new and evolving business enterprises that see social, human and environmental benefits to be just as important as making a profit. Using disruptive technologies such as the electronic and dematerialised forms discussed earlier, and engaging with multiple stakeholders, these enterprises may well represent new ways for people to express their humanity and their dreams—as well as new forms of enterprise providing the basis of the creative destruction that Schumpeter (1962) argued is how capitalism shifts.

There is still significant inertia in the present system despite the economic upheaval of 2008. But SEE Change suggests there are disruptive enterprises poised to unseat powerful interests from below. Further, as many of the companies discussed earlier have already demonstrated, new technologies and new, sometimes more democratic, approaches can be successful.

Although there is a long way to go for that to happen, and many entrenched interests that would work to prevent it, the very connectivity that is fostering these emergent enterprises may enable them, ultimately, to make a significant impact. Many of these new SEE Change enterprises carry a very different mindset from traditional corporations which have been described as nothing short of psychopathic in the way they are constructed and designed (Bakan 2004). At the same time, many good people work in today's larger business enterprises and are already working hard to embed sustainability and responsibility practices in their companies.

Below, we will explore new forms of business enterprise that are now emerging and that are explicitly designed with a multiple-bottom-line imperative at their core. Like the redesign of the corporate form discussed in Chapter 4 in the section on Corporation 2020, these SEE Change enterprises integrate profits, society and ecology. A number of movements and collectivities are attempting to define them, including for-benefit and B corporations, the conscious capitalism movement and the fourth sector, not to mention attempts to build nature-based products based on biomimicry. Other, more traditional forms that have more democratic forms of governance than traditional corporations, such as ESOPs (employee share ownership plans) and cooperatives, can be found alongside these emerging new types.

Three interesting developments in recent years are the for-benefit corporation, the B corporation, and a nascent conscious capitalism movement. These types of business enterprises explicitly take social and ecological considerations into account in their business strategies and purposes.

For-benefit corporations

A corporate innovation, and perhaps simultaneously a form of social entrepreneurship, is the 'for-benefit corporation', a term apparently coined by the *New York Times* in talking about a company called Altrushare in 2007. Altrushare is a brokerage firm in which two charities jointly own a controlling interest. It is an example of what the *Times* called 'the emerging convergence of for-profit money-making and non-profit missions' (Strom 2007). The International Finance Corporation picked up on the term, arguing that it had been supporting emerging 'for-benefit' companies for years, but without the label, as a way of developing emerging markets.[7]

Although some economists, such as Michael Jensen (2000), argue that companies (or any enterprise) can serve only one master, or what Jensen terms 'one objective function' (typically profit-maximising), the idea behind for-benefit, B corporations and fourth sector enterprise more generally is that it is indeed possible for companies to successfully negotiate multiple bottom lines. A growing array of social entrepreneurs around the world is proving Jensen's assertion incorrect, as they are successfully navigating between the two worlds of doing well financially *and* doing good for the world.

B Corporations

In an interesting development aligned with the concept of the for-benefit corporation, a group of companies in the US recently agreed to change their governance documents and become B corporations. A group of 81 pioneering, mostly relatively small companies, including Seventh Generation, Trillium Asset Management and White Dog Café founded B Corporation with the intent of trying to provide consumers with access to information about branded companies that are certified as actually having met specific criteria related to CR. At the time of writing, B Corporation had 255 members holding more than US$1.1 billion in revenues and covering 54 industries (see Boxes 1 and 2).[8]

A B corporation attempts to live up to transparent, comprehensive social and environmental standards by building these values into companies' governing documents. They also incorporate stakeholders' not just

---

7 ifcblog.ifc.org/emergingmarketsifc/2007/06/forbenefit_corp.html, accessed 28 April 2009.

8 www.bcorporation.net, accessed 4 February 2010.

shareholders' interests into their core governance structure and purposes. By bringing together stakeholder interests they hope to 'build collective voice through the power of a unifying brand'.

B Corporation created what it calls a Declaration of Interdependence that frames its mission. This Declaration states:[9]

> That we must be the change we seek in the world. That all business ought to be conducted as if people and place mattered. That, through their products, practices and profits, businesses should aspire to do no harm and benefit all. To do so requires that we act with the understanding that we are each dependent upon another and thus responsible for each other and future generations.

In 2009, *Business Week* published a list of 25 of 'America's most promising social entrepreneurs'. On that list were seven of the B Corporation companies (Perman *et al.* 2009).

Box 1 **King Arthur Flour**

The more than 200-year-old American flour company, King Arthur Flour, is a 100% employee-owned company committed to 'producing the best bag of flour available'. It has been named one of the *Wall Street Journal*'s Top Small Workplaces. The New England company's employee ownership model provides an explicit stake for all employees in the business's success. The company supports employee volunteerism with 40 hours of paid leave for service activities and has a stewardship team devoted to local and in-house sustainability. King Arthur prides itself on earning respect for its core values, for its honest enthusiasm about the business, for its culture of inclusiveness, and because it views profits and wealth creation as 'inevitable by-products of doing things well'.[10] King Arthur Flour is a member of B Corporation.

---

9 B Corporation, 'Declaration of Interdependence', www.bcorporation.net/ declaration, accessed 28 April 2009.

10 Further information from www.bcorporation.net/kingarthurflour and www. kingarthurflour.com/about, accessed 4 February 2010.

Box 2 **Seventh Generation**

Seventh Generation, a B Corporation member, produces natural and non-toxic household and personal care products. The company is committed to ensuring that all of its products are sustainable, including raw materials, by-products and production processes. It works closely with suppliers and other partners to improve ingredient transparency and traceability, to educate retailers about products' environmental impacts through its GIVE (Generate Inspiration Via Education) programme, and is involved in a continual improvement process both for itself and the world around it.[11]

Conscious capitalism

Another development—deliberately designed as a movement—is the nascent conscious capitalism movement,[12] which argues that a 'conscious business' rests on three core principles:

- **Deeper purpose**: Recognising that every business has a deeper purpose than merely profit maximisation, a conscious business is clear about, and focused on, fulfilling its deeper purpose;

- **Stakeholder model**: A conscious business focuses on delivering value to all its stakeholders, and works to align and harmonise the interests of customers, employees, suppliers, investors, the community and the environment to the greatest extent possible;

- **Conscious leadership**: In a conscious business, management embodies conscious leadership and fosters it throughout the organisation. Conscious leaders serve as stewards to the company's deeper purpose and its stakeholders, focusing on fulfilling the company's purpose, delivering value to its stakeholders and facilitating a harmony of interests, rather than merely personal gain and self-aggrandisement. Conscious leaders cultivate awareness throughout their business ecosystem, beginning with themselves and their team members, and moving into their relationships with each other and other stakeholders.

11 www.bcorporation.net/seventhgeneration, accessed 4 February 2010.
12 consciouscapitalism.com/?page_id=59, accessed 4 February 2010.

C3, or Catalyzing Conscious Capitalism, was co-founded by Whole Foods CEO (see Box 3) John Mackey to help create and deepen the conscious capitalism movement so that more enterprises could join Whole Foods, The Container Store, Joie de Vivre Hotels and REI, among others, in achieving these goals.

C3 provides a rationale for choosing the term conscious capitalism:[13]

> The choice of the term 'conscious capitalism' has been made after considerable thought. We believe this term best captures the depth and complexity of the changes in the business-operating model that are needed. It reflects the fact that more people today are at higher levels of consciousness about themselves and the world around them than ever before. This is due in part to natural evolution, but also to the rapid ageing of society, which has resulted in a higher proportion of people in midlife and beyond, when consciousness is raised and higher-level needs predominate. The advent of the Internet has accelerated and cemented this trend, simultaneously connecting hundreds of millions of people and placing great demands for transparency on companies.

Box 3 **Whole Foods**

Whole Foods Market was founded in Austin, Texas in 1980 and has become the world's leader in natural and organic foods. With more the 270 stores in the US and the UK, Whole Foods emphasises strict quality standards for its natural and organic products, and a commitment to sustainable agriculture. The company has grown both internally and through acquisitions of other organic and natural foods purveyors. As a mission-driven business, the company attempts to integrate three core strategic areas: whole foods; whole people; and whole planet. Whole Foods maintains a list of core values that reflect what it views as important: 'selling the highest quality natural and organic products available, satisfying and delighting our customers, supporting team member happiness and excellence, creating wealth through profits and growth, caring about our communities and environment, creating on-going win-win partnerships with our suppliers, and promoting the health of our stakeholders through healthy eating education'.[14]

13 consciouscapitalism.com/?page_id=44, accessed 4 February 2010.
14 www.wholefoodsmarket.com/company/index.php, accessed 4 February 2010.

Biomimicry

One orientation for SEE Change is the emerging discipline of biomimicry which 'studies nature's best ideas and then imitates these designs and processes to solve human problems'.[15] According to Benyus (2002), bio-mimicry focuses on designs based in nature to create products, processes and even organisations and policies that are sustainable and adapted to their environment. The premise is that nature 'knows best', and that by imitating nature human enterprise can be creative in a significantly more sustainable way.

While companies actually producing things through biomimicry tech-niques are still few in number, Benyus argues that such approaches, even though difficult to achieve, could produce results that avoid the toxic chemicals and resource-intensive manufacturing methods employed in much modern manufacturing. Existing examples include velcro (which uses the way that burrs stick to things to create a zipper-like fastener), gecko tape (a tape covered with tiny hairs like those on geckos to create a potent adhesive) and self-healing plastics (that use polymer compos-ite hollow fibres filled with epoxy that is released if the fibres are stressed or cracked to reseal a tear, much as the body heals a wound). Another product, which helped US swimmer Michael Phelps achieve his Olympic triumph of eight medals in Beijing in 2008, is the Speedo Fastskin FSII swimsuit which is based on shark skin's ability to reduce drag.

Enterprises of the future

While most of the enterprises discussed in this chapter are still relatively small, especially when compared to multinational corporations, we believe that collectively they may represent the future—the force of crea-tive destruction—which can potentially unseat the behemoths that cur-rently exist. Part of their strength lies in their sense of purpose which can create passion and energy among employees, customers and even inves-tors. In addition, they can potentially use their innovative technologies and capacity for connectivity to bring new ideas and people together in origi-nal ways. It is this type of capacity that is the essence of creative destruc-tion. As we will see in Chapter 6, these emergent forms and approaches

15 www.biomimicry.net, accessed 5 February 2010.

to business are not the only shifts that have potential to reshape the way humans connect, do business and live their lives. The very technological advances that have made possible some of these businesses are also blurring sector and organisational boundaries in other important ways.

6

Social entrepreneurship
Crossing sector boundaries

As we saw in the last chapter, many businesses are being formed or are reconstituting themselves on principles that combine social, environmental and economic goals. Further, there is a growing prevalence of multi-sector collaborative enterprises that cross increasingly blurred sector boundaries. The 'wicked problems' (Churchman 1967) of sustainability, climate change, poverty, economic and social development, food production, human security and others have created a glaring need for more organisations to reach across traditional sector boundaries and purposes. These entities, which are attempting to solve the 'messes' (Ackoff 1975) or wicked problems, have resulted in the emergence of what is being called the 'fourth sector'.[1] In addition, the blurring boundaries have spawned a growing array of enterprises that are classed as social enterprises or socially entrepreneurial organisations. Some of these organisations have been described as 'hybrid' because they have a variety of organisational forms and link organisations from what were regarded as very different, or even opposing, sectors. This chapter will explore these emerging types of SEE Change enterprises and some of their characteristics.

1 www.fourthsector.net, accessed 4 February 2010.

The fourth sector

The fourth sector labelling recognises the blurring of boundaries that has occurred in many types of enterprises, particularly around what Jed Emerson (2003) has called the 'blended value proposition' of making profits while simultaneously serving a social and/or ecological purpose. The Fourth Sector is a coalition of multi-sector leaders from a wide variety of enterprises focused on developing a fourth sector of society. Fourth Sector's website and first report notes, as we have above, that boundaries between public and private enterprise are, and have for some time been, blurring.[2] In this context, Fourth Sector's founder Heerad Sabati points out that many companies, including numerous large corporations, are engaging in a wide array of activities that have social purpose as well as profit-making potential, as discussed in Chapter 5. Among the efforts that large companies are engaged in are, among others: CSR; cause-related marketing and purchasing; carbon offset programmes; corporate philanthropy; environmental management and sustainability programmes; community relations; SRI and triple-bottom-line approaches; stakeholder accountability; and sustainability reporting.[3]

But because the power, resources and interests of large corporations are relatively entrenched, with significant momentum to continue to focus predominantly on profits and wealth maximisation without necessarily referencing social or ecological goals, it will be difficult to transform them to meet the needs of the 21st century. Implicitly following Schumpeter's (1962) theory of creative destruction, Fourth Sector highlights the surge in new types of enterprises that have begun—from inception or soon thereafter—to cross sector, goal and organisational boundaries.

Enterprises of the fourth sector go by many labels and involve many different types of what are called 'hybrid' organisations and enterprises—hybrid because they do not neatly fit traditional categories of private, non-profit/NGO or governmental organisations. We have already discussed B corporations, for-benefit corporations and the CR initiatives of many large corporations in the last two chapters—all important elements of SEE Change. To this list, we can add other labels for hybrid organisations, some of which are dominantly business oriented but with underlying social purposes—social enterprises; chaordic organisations; sustainable

---

2 www.fourthsector.net/learn, accessed 10 February 2010.
3 www.fourthsector.net/learn/fourth-sector, accessed 4 February 2010.

enterprises; blended value organisations; new profit companies; common good corporations; and social businesses.

Because fourth sector enterprises blend purposes, however, their value proposition is, by definition, mixed. There are also numerous types of entities broadly labelled social enterprises that arise initially from the perspective of other sectors, including non-profit enterprises, community wealth enterprises, ethical social institutions, faith-based enterprises, civic/municipal enterprises, community-interest organisations and community development corporations. Further, there are numerous cross-sector partnerships, multi-sector collaborations and related multiple sector enterprises working to achieve common good purposes, some of which are what Waddell and Khagram call GANs (global action networks), which will be discussed in the next chapter.[4]

Similarly, many NGOs or CSOs are engaging in business-related practices to improve their performance, becoming more businesslike in the process. For example, NGOs frequently engage in defining measurable impact, using market discipline to harness their energy, and employing efficiency and accountability methods developed by business. They also sometimes try to develop profit-making ventures to ensure economic viability, or engage in social investment activities. Generally, as they attempt to become more efficient and effective in achieving their social mission, NGOs are finding it advantageous to use more business-like approaches, including, at times, profit-making activities that can bolster the bottom-line.

Fourth Sector emphasises the proliferation of new types of enterprise that it classifies as hybrids between public and private enterprise. Such entities, according to Fourth Sector, 'resist easy classification within the boundaries of the three traditional sectors. But they share two common characteristics—pursuit of social and environmental aims and the use of business methods.'[5] These characteristics are also typical of SEE Change enterprises of which the emerging fourth sector is certainly a part.

The argument that Fourth Sector makes is that the blending of value in all of these enterprises is actually constructing a new—fourth—sector that differs from the traditional three sectors or spheres of business/economics, government/public policy and civil society (see Waddock 2009)

---

4 GAN is a construct jointly developed by Steve Waddell and Rajeev Khagram. More information can be found at www.scalingimpact.net/gan, accessed 27 April 2009.

5 www.fourthsector.net/learn/fourth-sector, accessed 28 April 2009.

because of the blended value proposition integral to these different types of enterprise (Emerson 2003). In what Fourth Sector terms a convergence of organisation into a 'new landscape that integrates social purposes with business methods', these hybrid organisations are rapidly evolving and creating new ways of dealing with the wicked problems that our world is facing (Sabati 2009).

The coalition that represents Fourth Sector, led by Heerad Sabati, has developed an archetype of the fourth sector enterprise, which they term the 'for-benefit organisation'. Characteristics of this type of enterprise are that it simultaneously pursues social purposes and business activities. The social purpose is embedded in its organisational structure, and the business simply needs to be consistent with its social purposes and stakeholder responsibilities (Sabati 2009: 5). In addition to these core elements, for-benefit organisations have other emergent tendencies—inclusive ownership; stakeholder governance; fair compensation; reasonable returns (versus maximised returns); transparency; and social–ecological responsibility (Sabati 2009: 5).

The Fourth Sector also notes that it will be difficult for fourth sector enterprises to evolve unless there is a supportive enterprise ecosystem for them. This supportive ecosystem includes new forms of bridging the gap between traditional for-profit and not-for-profit status, and legal and regulatory structures that fully sanction such enterprises (with the possibility that new legal contracts may need to be created). Tax policies and laws that reward such enterprises may also need to be developed.

Other facilitating elements of this new fourth sector ecosystem include training for those individuals who would start such enterprises, and new approaches to conflict resolution, particularly since fourth sector enterprises frequently involve stakeholders (including customers and employees) more democratically than traditional organisations. Marketing approaches will shift with these enterprises, as authenticity is key to their effectiveness (for example, when Kiva (see Box 8) was perceived to go against its foundational principles many questions were raised about whether it was being true to its mission and origins).

Fourth Sector also points out that the alliances and relationships with other entities such as membership networks, trade associations and affinity groups, further complicates the ecosystem in which fourth sector enterprises exist, and that much more needs to be learned about how these types of enterprises develop and operate effectively, as well as how their trustworthiness and credibility can be assessed and transparently reported (Sabati 2009: 6-7). Even the way that value is created and exchanged, the type of logistical and other support needed may differ in these types of enterprises in the longer run as they evolve and develop. Boxes 1–3 provide brief examples of some emerging fourth sector enterprises.

Box 1 **Grameen Danone Foods**

The Grameen Bank, discussed in the section on micro-loans and micro-enterprise, has extended its reach to numerous businesses beyond micro-lending, including healthcare, education, telecommunications, textiles, information systems, renewable energy, water and fisheries, among many others.[6] As part of its expansion, Grameen has begun partnering with large corporations, one of which is the French group Danone, a leader in dairy products.[7] The Grameen Danone Foods collaboration was begun in 2006 with the intention of improving the health of the 30–56% of Bangladeshi children who suffer from malnutrition. Founded as a joint venture, Grameen Danone produces a special enriched yoghurt at a price affordable for even the poorest families. Extending the benefits, Grameen Danone purchases milk for the yoghurt from local micro-farmers as a means of providing as many jobs locally as possible, and uses local women to sell and distribute the product, which is packaged in biodegradable containers. As of 2010, the collaboration had created some 1,600 jobs in a 30 mile radius of the manufacturing plant.[8]

Box 2 **Cafédirect**

Cafédirect is a pioneering fair trade producer and seller of coffee that arose out of the ashes of the collapse of the International Coffee Agreement in 1989. It began when coffee growers in Peru, Costa Rica and Mexico decided to each ship one container of coffee to the UK—on trust. Local charities and church groups roasted and sold the beans—and the rest, as they say, is history. Established before the Fairtrade Foundation in the UK, Cafédirect now carries that label and, in 2004, became a publicly listed company in the UK by raising £5 million from some 4,500 investors. Cafédirect is a product of a collaboration by Oxfam, Equal Exchange, Traidcraft and Twin Trading who collectively determined to buy coffee directly

6 www.grameencreativelab.com/a-concept-to-eradicate-poverty/grameen-the-mother-of-social-business.html, accessed 15 February 2010.

7 www.danone.com/?lang=en, accessed 15 February 2010.

8 www.grameencreativelab.com/live-examples/grameen-danone-foods-ltd.html, accessed 15 February 2010.

from disadvantaged growers in developing countries, avoiding the costs of 'middle men'. By working directly with coffee growers, Cafédirect is able to put more than 50% of its profits back into the growers' businesses. Now the UK's largest 100% fair trade hot drinks company, Cafédirect claims to positively affect the lives of 1.6 million people in 14 countries through its production of coffees, teas and hot chocolates, which are sold in fair trade outlets as well as major supermarkets and other retailers. The company's growers now can be found in Africa (Cameroon, Kenya, Rwanda, Tanzania and Uganda), Latin America (Costa Rica, Haiti, Mexico, Nicaragua and Peru) and Asia (India and Sri Lanka).[9]

Box 3 **WikiHow**

One unusual type of fourth sector enterprise is represented by WikiHow, a web-based enterprise with a mission, 'to build the world's largest and most accurate how-to manual', with free instructions on 'how to do' just about anything.[10] Claiming itself as a hybrid organisation, WikiHow was established independently in 2006. By 2010 it had more than 72,000 freely available 'how to' articles ranging from tyre changing to avoiding traffic jams. Structured like Wikipedia, WikiHow invites contributors to, 'share your how-to with millions of people', who can then edit and improve the contributed articles. The website is supported by advertising. Entered content is licensed by another non-profit enterprise, Creative Commons, which is 'dedicated to helping copyright holders be able to distribute and share their work on the web', by creating licensing agreements specifically designed by the copyright holder (with options ranging from public domain, by attribution, share-alike [which allows for sharing of resources in derivative works, no derivatives allowed and non-commercial distribution permitted]).[11]

---

9 www.cafedirect.co.uk/index.cfm, accessed 15 February 2010.
10 www.aboutus.org/wikiHow.com, accessed 15 February 2010.
11 www.aboutus.org/CreativeCommons.org, accessed 15 February 2010.

Social enterprises and social entrepreneurs

Fourth sector enterprises are an emerging organisational form that starts with social purposes and incorporates business purposes and approaches. There are also emerging enterprises that are largely business enterprises but which are deliberately established for social benefit. Such enterprises are also sometimes labelled 'social enterprises'—and they are started by individuals who are social entrepreneurs. Fourth sector enterprises of all sorts deliberately cross boundaries at their inception, while social enterprises frequently arise within a sector and then cross boundaries as they evolve their purposes. Conceptually, and in practice, however, there is a good deal of overlap among what might be labelled fourth sector enterprises and what have been called social enterprises or social entrepreneurial organisations. While we believe that these 'types' are conceptually quite similar, and may eventually assume a single designation, because social enterprises have received a good deal of publicity we deal with them separately here. One difference is that profit may or may not be a motivating factor for social enterprises, even while business methods and approaches, and fee-for-service charges or other revenue-producing initiatives may be used.

Social entrepreneurship from within big corporations

Social enterprises are often thought of as mission-driven businesses with multiple (or at least dual) bottom-lines of profitability, and some sort of social or ecological benefit. In social enterprises, the mission serves some social and/or sustainability purpose, typically in addition to generating enough profits to at least sustain the entity and, often, to make money in the same way as traditional business enterprises. Social enterprises can be for-profit or not-for-profit, which means they do not distribute profits to owners as there are, typically, no owners of not-for-profits. But social enterprises often have, at minimum, the dual objectives of being profitable or balancing their budgets while also seeking beneficial social change. They also tend to use business approaches to accomplish their objectives as opposed to the less structured 'social good' approaches used by many purely charitable organisations.[12]

12 'Social Enterprise Typology', www.4lenses.org/setypology, accessed 8 February 2009.

Many so-called 'bottom of the pyramid' (also known as 'base of the pyramid') enterprises are social enterprises. The term 'bottom of the pyramid' comes from the work of C.K. Prahalad who published a book by that name in 2005 (Prahalad 2005; see also Prahalad and Hammond 2002). Corporate strategist Stuart Hart has also written extensively on how to solve the world's problems through social entrepreneurship (Hart 1997, 2005a). Prahalad argued that there was a fortune to be made by companies who engaged in business with the four to five billion people at the 'bottom-of-the-pyramid' (BoP) that is, who are living in significant levels of poverty. He argued that, starting with respect for the poor as individuals, companies can and should use creative and innovative approaches, such as what Clayton Christensen and co-authors have called catalytic or disruptive innovations for social change (Christensen *et al.* 2006).

The Christensen approach, which is based on his earlier work on disruptive innovations, suggests that catalytic *social* change has five qualities. Catalytic social entrepreneurs create systemic social change through scaling and replication. They meet a need that is either over-served (i.e. the existing solution is more complex/expensive than people need) or not served at all. They offer products and services that are simpler and less costly than existing alternatives (and may have lower performance perceptions too), but are seen as good enough by their target customers. Further, such catalytic social changes generate resources (donations, grants, volunteers, intellectual capital) in ways which are initially unattractive to incumbent competitors, and are often ignored, disparaged or even encouraged by existing players (because the business model would be unprofitable for them).

Not all social entrepreneurship, of course, is disruptive in the sense that Christensen discusses. Some of it is aimed simply at meeting previously unmet needs among the poor or otherwise unserved populations. Prahalad argues against assumptions that people on low incomes do not spend money on goods and services, or that barriers such as corruption, illiteracy and lack of infrastructure too frequently cause businesses to avoid the large population of people mired in poverty. He considers this view to be out-dated, pointing out that many corporations do, in fact, serve this population. Particularly in aggregate, the buying power of the BoP population is quite large, and meeting the needs of this market for low-priced, reasonable quality goods could enhance revenues (Prahalad and Hammond 2002).

Although some critics question whether the market is, in fact, as large as Prahalad has argued (Karnani 2007), nonetheless there has been an explosion of interest in social entrepreneurship. As with Christensen's approach, Prahalad suggests that strategies for large corporations attempting to serve the BoP involve thinking more creatively, over-coming assumptions that the market is fundamentally flawed, educating managers to the opportunities in the market and focusing business development specifically at these markets. Making alliances with local entrepreneurs (especially women), changing internal structures to accommodate the differences in BoP markets, and dealing with local difficulties related to infrastructure, connectivity and corruption also need to be handled carefully (Prahalad and Hammond 2002; Hart 2005b). See Box 4 on KickStart for an example of social entrepreneurship.

Box 4 **KickStart**

KickStart is an NGO focused on developing and marketing new technologies that can help local entrepreneurs in Kenya and elsewhere create and manage small enterprises. Its mission is to 'help millions of people out of poverty' by promoting 'sustainable economic growth and employment creation'.[13] KickStart helps entrepreneurs identify new business opportunities, access needed technologies and capitalise these technologies at between US$100 and $1,000. The seeds of KickStart lie in an enterprise called ApproTEC, founded in 1991, which became KickStart in 2005. Working through a five-step process, KickStart helps people identify business opportunities, design products and tools that will make the business possible, establish a relevant supply chain, develop the market, and assess and evaluate progress. A technologically based organisation, KickStart uses a design team of engineers, designers and technicians based in Nairobi, Kenya, for the development and testing of prototypes that are culturally appropriate. Key to the success of KickStart is the development of a sustainable supply chain for the tools that are produced, since KickStart buys back the manufactured tools and then creates a local wholesale, distribution and retail chain, with community-based, profit-motivated entrepreneurs throughout the supply chain. One product is the Money-Maker Pump, sold to over 91,000 entrepreneurs to help them deal with water issues. KickStart estimates that it takes an investment of around US$300 to bring a single family out of poverty, and new products are introduced at a loss until a tipping point is reached at which the market is built and the product becomes profitable.

---

13 www.kickstart.org/about-us, accessed 15 February 2010.

Social entrepreneurship from start-ups

Social enterprises begin and grow in much the same way as typical entrepreneurial ventures—from the ground up, starting as small start-ups and sometimes staying small, but at other times becoming much larger. The people who start these ventures are often called social entrepreneurs, a term that gained popularity through the work of Bill Drayton, founder of Ashoka (see next section), which bills itself as the 'global association of the world's leading social entrepreneurs—men and women with system-changing solutions for the world's most urgent social problems'.[14]

The purposes of social enterprises tend to lean towards meeting some social or ecological need that the founding social entrepreneurs believed to be in the public interest or common good. Generally, they fit what might be characterised as progressive agendas. Many are focused on sustainability as well as positive social change; for instance, efforts to reduce poverty or create entrepreneurial activities among the poor through business activities can be viewed as social entrepreneurship, as can efforts to create businesses that serve otherwise unmet real needs or enhance sustainability. Unlike governmental bodies, however, social enterprises reflect the beliefs and motivations of the founding entrepreneurs themselves. They are not elected representatives of the public and, in that sense, their orientation towards the 'public good' is based on whatever definition of 'public good' they themselves apply.

Social entrepreneurs

The classic definition of social entrepreneurs, by Gregory Dees (1998), are of individuals who play the role of change agents in the social sector, by:

- Adopting a mission to create and sustain social value (not just private value);

- Recognising and relentlessly pursuing new opportunities to serve that mission;

- Engaging in a process of continuous innovation, adaptation and learning;

- Acting boldly without being limited by resources currently in hand;

14 ashoka.org, accessed 11 February 2010.

- Exhibiting a heightened sense of accountability to the constituencies served and for the outcomes created.

Social entrepreneurs are, in some senses, simply entrepreneurs with traditional characteristics of opportunity sensing, out-of-the-box thinking and determination (Martin and Osberg 2007). As entrepreneurs, they combine *inspiration* to change something that needs improving with the *creativity* to develop new solutions to old problems—something that others have not thought of before. Further, social entrepreneurs are *action-oriented risk-takers* who do not wait for others to solve a problem, but step into the fray themselves. They are prepared to take whatever risks are needed to move their purpose forward, which takes courage, persistence and fortitude.

The differentiation between social and traditional entrepreneurs is that social entrepreneurs are driven by the 'passionate desire to deal with social problems', not necessarily for altruistic reasons as might commonly be assumed, but instead 'focusing on the social benefits' that will accrue from the innovation (Martin and Osberg 2007: 34). Notable in this definition is the emphasis on *changing* the social order inherent in social entrepreneurship.

Based on these ideas, we can say that social entrepreneurs are creative problem-solvers who are mission driven and focused on creating social value out of problems that currently exist: they are persistent, passionate and purposeful in fulfilling that mission incrementally in a process of continuous improvement and innovation, unlimited by (lack of) resources and accountable to their stakeholders. Social entrepreneurs inspired by the thought of positive social change, who see opportunities in social (and environmental) problems that others have not. They tend to be driven by values that emphasise working towards a better world rather than material gain, are persistent, passionate and purposeful in pursuing their agenda through action-oriented risk-taking, and remain accountable to their stakeholders. As Dees (1998) points out, they also act boldly without being limited by current (or no) resources.

Social entrepreneurship and enterprise

Through its Ashoka Fellows programme, Ashoka has supported more than 2,000 social entrepreneurships with stipends, professional development and networking opportunities. According to Ashoka, social entrepreneurs are 'ambitious and persistent, tackling major social issues and offering new ideas for wide-scale change'.[15] Ashoka views social entrepreneurs as passionate system changers who 'often seem possessed by their ideas, committing their lives to changing the direction of their field. They are both visionaries and ultimate realists, concerned with the practical implementation of their vision above all else.'

The enterprises created by social entrepreneurs emerge in a variety of different ways. Some, as discussed above, are divisions or initiatives that are created in large multinational corporations because the company believes it can 'do well by doing good;' that is, it can make a profit while serving some unmet social or ecological need or niche. Others are formed as entrepreneurial ventures and are designed from their inception to have the dual purpose of profits and social purpose. In some places, entities that serve social needs, such as credit unions, associations and cooperatives, are also considered to be social enterprises. Increasingly, non-profit organisations are engaging in money-making activities that generate profits as a means of supporting their social goals, and sometimes these too are classified as social enterprises. Social enterprises are founded or initiated within larger entities by social entrepreneurs, who have certain general characteristics.

Social enterprise within NGOs or as non-profit enterprises

Social enterprise also takes place increasingly inside non-profit organisations, NGOs and CSOs, when they attempt to provide a stable source of income for their mission- or values-driven activities by developing an internal business model. David Bornstein, after documenting the impressive growth in NGOs in recent times, argues that these so-called independent, third or not-for-profit sector enterprises should be labelled 'citizen sector enterprises' (Bornstein 2007). Social entrepreneurs starting from the citizen sector increasingly need to adopt business models to sustain their businesses, even while they do not seek profits in the traditional sense.

To provide a steady source of income, for example, some social enterprises might create a business within the larger entity (e.g. selling supplies or other goods to provide a regular income without having to rely on grants). Others create a business model that brings in resources, but does not aim to make a profit as such, just capacity for survival. Boxes 5 and 6 provide illustrations of some of this type of activity.

---

15 ashoka.org/social_entrepreneur, accessed 11 February 2010.

Box 5 **Invennovations**

Invennovations is an NGO that bills itself as 'putting the access puzzle together for the base of the pyramid'.[16] Designed to 'capture and disseminate the inventions and innovations being created and implemented around the world to serve vulnerable populations', Invennovations provides support to field workers in developing countries, trying to improve the lot of people at the BoP. Attempting to correct inefficiencies in design and distribution of products and technologies to this population, Invennovations is part of the New Development Solutions group, an umbrella for several agencies working on health, economic and education problems for the targeted populations. The NGO works through a website in which it lists the 'invennovations' already developed so that other inventors and innovators, including strategic partners, can access them by category. The website lists the characteristics of the invennovations, such as targeted beneficiaries, needs addressed, a description of the invennovation, its uniqueness, physical characteristics, and the innovator's name and contact information, among other pieces of information. Invennovations can be in any number of categories, including alternative fuels, computers, energy and lighting, medical, oral rehydration, housing, stoves and cookers, water pumps, and many others that in various ways serve the needs of the very poor.

Box 6 **Digital Data Divide**

Digital Data Divide (DDD)[17] is a multiple-bottom-line business focused on the data needs of publishers, libraries, content hosts, academic researchers and businesses on a global basis, creating more searchable and accessible information online. But it is more than an internet-based information company that serves clients around the world. DDD has an equal commitment to a social mission that 'creates opportunity for the world's poorest citizens to earn competitive wages, complete their education, and achieve upward mobility through working in our business'. DDD has trained some 1,500 people with marketable skills, it employs more than 600, and it helps to shape leaders out of young people born into impoverished situations in Cambodia and Laos by educating and training them for three to eight months in basic computer and English skills, then hiring them if they meet the company's standards. Once they are trained, recruits provide IT services for the company's global clients, enabling them to support their

16 www.invennovations.com, accessed 15 February 2010.
17 www.digitaldividedata.org, accessed 15 February 2010.

families and work towards earning a degree. After graduation, the recruits typically obtain good jobs, earning as much as six times the typical local wage. By 2010, some 250 staff had made this transition to employment in other companies.

Micro-enterprise and micro-finance

One of the interesting advances made in recent years has been the development of micro-finance approaches to fund small businesses and entrepreneurs, particularly in developing countries where such approaches are used to try to bring people out of extreme poverty. Micro-finance or micro-credit is premised on making quite small loans to entrepreneurs, frequently women, with little collateral, but who are willing to participate in a peer-based support and repayment network. The idea behind micro-finance was pioneered by Muhammad Yunus who, with Grameen Bank,[18] won the Nobel Peace Prize in 2006. Providing small loans, mostly to women, enables participants to fund small businesses from which they can earn enough to lift themselves and their families out of grinding poverty.

Grameen is perhaps the world's best known micro-finance agency, but its approaches have since been adopted by the UN and numerous other agencies to forward the entrepreneurship and small business efforts of poor people. In founding Grameen Bank, Yunus understood that conventional banking practices would be too costly, so he created a system of local support based on the belief that credit is a basic human right that should foster human potential for growth, rather than relying on conventional thinking that fundamentally rests on the principle that 'the more you have, the more you can get'.[19]

As a leading micro-finance bank, Grameen now serves more than 8 million borrowers (of which 97% are women), has more than 2,500 branches and serves more than 80,000 villages in Bangladesh. Grameen operates at the local level by providing very small loans to local entrepreneurs, organ-

18 www.grameen.com, accessed 12 February 2010.
19 Grameen Bank, 'Is Grameen Bank Different?' www.grameen-info.org/index. php?option=com_content&task=view&id=27&Itemid=176, accessed 12 February 2010.

ising small groups of them into networks to ensure repayment. In contrast to conventional banking, Grameen's focus is on women, in the belief that they will use resources gained from their business to provide food, shelter, clothing and opportunities for their children. It operates predominantly in small villages and rural areas, bringing banking services to village people, with repayment occurring weekly in small instalments. Combining social, anti-poverty and economic development objectives along with profitability goals, Grameen—and other micro-finance entities—has a 97% repayment rate, far better than traditional loan repayment rates.

Today there are many types of micro-finance institutions (MFIs), mostly supporting various forms of micro-enterprise. Most of these, like Grameen Bank, provide very small, non-collateralised loans to the very poor. Sometimes, MFIs are run as for-profit entities since repayment rates tend to be very good, while others are organised as credit unions, financial cooperatives, state-owned development agencies and, sometimes, postal services.[20] Sometimes, micro-loans and micro-credit are criticised because of their high interest rates (which can range from as low as 4% to as much as 50%), and for not bringing people totally out of poverty (Dichter 2007). Interest rates tend to be high because of the cost of administering numerous small loans, the need for loan officers to be present in many villages on a regular basis to ensure repayment, and because of related factors that mean that micro-finance tends to be a costly service.

Despite these criticisms, there is evidence that access to micro-loans reduces the vulnerability of loan recipients to the ill effects of poverty, reduces financial insecurity and enhances the consistency of their income flows (Murdoch 1998). Other studies suggest different benefits, such as more family income and quality of life, promoting habits of saving, raising awareness, and empowering and motivating women to participate more actively in civic activities (Islam 2009).[21] Boxes 7, 8 and 9 provide examples associated with micro-lending, and illustrate some of the variety found among these lenders.

---

20 www.microfinancegateway.org/p/site/m/template.rc/1.26.9183, accessed 12 February 2010.

21 K.F. Ahmed, 'Micro-credit as a Tool for Women Empowerment: The Case of Bangladesh', Foreign AID Ratings, www.foreignaid.com/thinktank/microcredit.html, accessed 12 February 2010,

Box 7 **Top MFIs**

In 2007 *Forbes* magazine published a list of the 'top 50' micro-credit institutions in the world, selected from 641 institutions.[22] The institutions were evaluated on the basis of scale (size of their gross loan portfolio), efficiency (operating expense and cost per borrower), risk and return. The top ten rankings went to ASA in Bangladesh, Bandhan in India, Banco do Nordeste in Brazil, Fundación Mundial de la Mujer Bucaramanga in Colombia, FONDEP Micro-Crédit in Morocco, Amhara Credit and Savings Institution in Ethiopia, Banco Compartamos, S.A., Institución de Banca Múlitple in Mexico, Association Al Amana for the Promotion of Micro-Enterprises Morocco, Fundación Mundo Mujer Popayán in Colombia and Fundación WWB Colombia–Cali. Grameen Bank was 17th on the list.

Box 8 **Kiva**

Kiva is a micro-lender that makes 'loans that save lives', with a mission 'to connect people, through lending, for the sake of alleviating poverty'.[23] Kiva uses a model of connecting lenders in developed nations with micro-entrepreneurs globally via the internet. As with Grameen, Kiva believes that people living in poverty are highly motivated to be successful if they are given a chance, that most people are generous and 'will help others if given the opportunity do so in a transparent, accountable way' and that the internet is a way of connecting people to create relationships that go beyond the financial transaction associated with lending.

Built on core values of dignity, accountability and transparency, Kiva operates through field partners located in places where loans are distributed. The partners are responsible for loan approval, disbursement and collection, and they also take photos of the entrepreneurs and details of their stories for display on Kiva's website. Lenders browse through entrepreneurs and choose someone to lend to (US$25 per person per entrepreneur), and funds are disbursed to the field partners, who make the actual loans. The entrepreneurs are expected to repay loans to the field partners, while lenders' loans can either be repaid or re-loaned once they are repaid.

---

22 'Top 50 Micro-finance Institutions', www.forbes.com/2007/12/20/microfinance-philanthropy-credit-biz-cz_ms_1220microfinance_table.html, accessed 12 February 2010.
23 www.kiva.org/about, accessed 15 February 2010.

Kiva's business model became somewhat controversial when it was revealed that loans did not go directly to entrepreneurs but rather through the field partner and when, in 2009, Kiva decided to make loans to US borrowers. Critics claimed that Kiva was supposed to be oriented towards the developing world and that loaning money to US borrowers 'undermined the very core of what made Kiva special'. Timothy Ogden, writing in *Harvard Business Online*, notes that the controversies highlight key aspects relevant to all social entrepreneurs: the need for truth in advertising; truth in impact; and the transparency of social media that surround such enterprises today.[24] Despite the controversies, as of early 2010, Kiva had made more than US$120 million loans via more than 670,000 lenders to nearly 300,000 entrepreneurs, with an impressive loan repayment rate of >98%.

Box 9 **Blue Orchard Finance**

Blue Orchard finance is a commercial micro-finance venture with a mission to 'empower the poor worldwide to participate in income-generating activities', using a variety of innovative financial products that invest in other micro-finance institutions, supporting millions of small enterprises while returning profitable returns for investors.[25] Unlike Kiva, Accion, Grameen and many other micro-lenders, Blue Orchard is a for-profit entity that focuses on bridging capital markets and micro-finance, by creating new investment instruments that allow investors to generate returns while still investing in micro-enterprise. The goal is not to directly support micro-entrepreneurs, but rather to support the infrastructure that allows investments to reach them, by providing credit and equity investments to MFIs. As with other blended value enterprises, Blue Orchard focuses both on the social impact and the quality of returns for its investors.

---

24 'Kiva's Cautionary Social Entrepreneurship Tale, www.businessweek.com/
   managing/content/oct2009/ca20091020_373698.htm, accessed 15 February 2010.
25 www.blueorchard.com/jahia/Jahia, accessed 15 February 2010.

People and their dreams

In a post-modern world of spin, anything goes, market-driven values and frenetic management styles, people are calling for enterprises founded on integrity and clear values. They are calling for organisations with purposes that go beyond maximising wealth for the already wealthy, and that focus on dealing with the multiple manifest problems of our world. They want organisations whose leaders have integrity and that operate with integrity. The social enterprises discussed in this and the last two chapters are trying to meet some of these shifting demands.

With integrity comes authenticity, truly doing what you say you do, as well as a capacity to reflect on the consequences of actions, which can be considered, wisdom about the choices being made (Ackoff 1999). This combination of authenticity and integrity at the workplace resonates with many who want to be able to bring their 'whole' selves to meaningful work in places whose purposes they fully understand and support. People typically want to work, since work is often a source of meaning and purposefulness in life. But too many places of work in our modern world are deeply dehumanising. We believe that SEE Change enterprises have the potential to change that situation. But they will require a different mind-set, approach and sense of purpose than are present in many of today's large organisations.

This new approach to enterprise rests on a need to go beyond simple problem-solving. There is a deep urgency for a renewed sense of hope and optimism about how to move the world forward, despite the poverty, overpopulation and social issues that surround us, despite the chaos of a failing economic system and collapsing ecological systems. Questions that emerge include: 'What does it mean to be in a humane and human-scale organisation?' 'How can communities that work *as* communities be built and sustained over time?' 'What changes need to happen that would allow people to actually *want* to go to work?' 'How do corporations need to change to fit into this equation?' 'What kind of world do we want to live in and leave for our grandchildren?' Ultimately, how do we connect with each other in wholly new ways which, as the social enterprises discussed in this chapter demonstrate, cross traditional boundaries? In the next chapter we will explore some other types of enterprises now emerging that cross sector boundaries even more radically, creating new networks of actors focused on constructive social change.

7
Boundary spanners

The world of clouds, crowds and virtual communities that we now live in is rapidly creating entirely new ways of relating to each other, and to the planet itself. As issues of environmental sustainability become paramount because of endangered ecosystems, people are finding new ways to connect. They are also finding new ways to create identity groups that can fracture the sense of the whole, while simultaneously crossing traditional boundaries—the subject of this chapter. The political scene in the US before and particularly since the economic meltdown of 2008 has become ever more divisive, making it harder to make policy decisions that are for the 'good of the whole'. Left and right appear more opposed than ever, and identity groups assume 'us versus them' attitudes that polarise communities and whole regions, not just in the US.

As long ago as 1990, Alvin Toffler wrote about some of the implications of a 'power shift' potentially creating increasing factionalism in the world along ethnic, religious, cultural and political lines (Toffler 1990). It seems that there are two opposing forces in contention—one forming identity groups that foster divisiveness and the other fostering a sense of the collective that has the potential to bring diverse people together on common issues. The US National Intelligence Council (NIC), for example, has forecast that, by 2025, there will be a multi-polar world with a rise of power by 'non-state actors', including businesses, tribes, religious organisations and criminal networks (NIC 2008).

The NIC report notes that power shifts will create more dispersion and that what we now think of as the international community comprised of nation states may no longer exist. Rather, power 'will be more dispersed, with the newer players bringing new rules of the game while risks will increase that traditional Western alliances will weaken.' Political and economic development models may also shift radically towards those of China and, possibly, other BRIC nations.[1] These countries are using a form of 'state capitalism' where governments or states play a more important role than in traditional 'laissez-faire' economic systems. This allocation of power to states is shifting the traditional boundaries associated with free market capitalism. This approach has been boosted by the 2008 economic collapse, as governments moved to save various businesses from their own highly risky or strategically misguided behaviours—moves that are likely to shift the boundaries between business and government for many years to come.

Other shifts on the global geopolitical scene are likely, the NIC report notes, including a shift in relative wealth from West to East, along with continuing and growing planetary strains on energy, food and water due to population growth, with climate change making these scarcities worse. Growing populations of jobless young people in some areas of the world (e.g. Afghanistan, Nigeria, Pakistan and Yemen) 'will remain ripe for continued instability and state failure', as well as ideological conflicts and terrorism, particularly if youth unemployment issues are not dealt with effectively. One possibility is a 'comeback' for mercantilism and 'resource nationalism', which could increase potential for confrontation among nations, along with the possibility of increased terrorism (NIC 2008).

The report further notes that while the international system is unlikely to break down completely, there are numerous risks ahead, with rivalries around trade, investments and technological innovations paramount. Power and profits are likely to shift to the BRIC nations, although the US is likely to remain a dominant force. Thus, geopolitical boundaries that have been in place since the end of World War II are shifting and will affect the way businesses operate in the future. In the context of what we are calling SEE Change, these geopolitical shifts suggest that radically new ways of coping with policy-making, connection and community, resources and innovation will be needed for humans and other species to thrive, and perhaps even to survive over the longer term.

Among the shifts that are occurring is a continuing growth in the prevalence of NGOs, such as the more than two million social justice and environment-oriented NGOs identified by Paul Hawken (2008). Tensions

---

1 Brazil, Russia, India and China.

between current dominant institutions with entrenched interests (e.g. the World Bank, IMF and WTO), and the more bottoms-up or grassroots approaches favoured by NGOs are likely. The NIC predicts major 'discontinuities, shocks and surprises'—pandemics, nuclear war and many others are possible.

In this shifting and risky context we have already seen the emergence of numerous initiatives that are crossing traditional boundaries in new ways. These emerging enterprises are using new connectivity and social media technologies to create virtual and actual businesses and communities for social and environmental benefit, as more traditional businesses struggle to catch up with emerging world of Web 2.0. Start-ups and smaller entities with multiple-bottom-line orientations stand in juxtaposition to entrenched interests in multinational and other large corporations, despite the moves of many of these larger entities to become more responsible and sustainable. These new entities will need support and, presumably, new regulatory and governance frameworks—sometimes on a global scale and sometimes at more local or national levels—to support them as they attempt to grow.

One of the notable features of the current landscape is the decided lack of workable global governance mechanisms. The UN is the world's only truly global institution. As a multilateral institution it attempts to bring together its 192 member nations to work towards international peace, security for all, friendly relations and international cooperation on human, social, cultural and humanitarian issues. Founded on principles of justice, human rights, dignity and fundamental freedoms, the UN attempts to harmonise the actions of nations to achieve these ends.[2]

The UN's role as world peacekeeper is complemented by the Bretton Woods institutions—IMF (international Monetary Fund), World Bank, WTO (World Trade Organisation) and IFC (International Finance Corporation)—which collectively have shaped and framed the global economic agenda since their inception after World War II (the WTO emerged in 1995 from meetings on the General Agreement on Tariffs and Trade). The WTO's focus is ensuring that trade among nations is free, predictable and smooth.[3] The IMF focuses on fostering global monetary cooperation, financial stability, international trade, high employment and sustainable economic growth, along with poverty reduction.[4] The World Bank provides

2 www.un.org/en/documents/charter/index.shtml, accessed 17 February 2010.
3 www.wto.org.
4 www.imf.org.

financial and technical assistance to developing countries, attempting to fight poverty and help countries improve by building capacity and partnerships between the public and private sector. It accomplishes its work through loans, credit and grants to developing nations for investment in education, health, public administration, infrastructure, financial and private sector development, agriculture and management of natural resources.[5]

The UN has been criticised as being highly bureaucratic and without sufficient enforcement capabilities to achieve its mission, especially in a highly fragmented and divisive world. In addition, the work of the Bretton Woods institutions has been challenged by many critics, who believe that their neoliberal agenda of 'free trade', loan and repatriation policies foster a divided world that enhances the power of the already rich states (and corporations), while putting developing nations at a disadvantage (Cavanagh *et al.* 2002; Perkins 2004, 2007, 2009).

This chapter will focus on some of the emerging institutional forms that are shaping the future landscape for businesses and other enterprises—not from the perspective of existing global institutions with their own agendas, but with the idea of generating new pressures and forces that shape the future of how business and other enterprises operate. One such entity that has received considerable press and grown to be the world's largest corporate citizenship initiative is the UN Global Compact.

At the inception of the UN Global Compact in 1999, Georg Kell (Executive Head of the Global Compact) and John Ruggie (then Special Assistant to the then UN Secretary-General Kofi Annan), who helped Annan found the Compact, noted that the forces of globalisation had shifted much of the global economic order that had been established after World War II by the Bretton Woods institutions and the UN. They argued that globalisation has created two disequilibria in the world environment, one between the economic sphere and the shared values and practices within which economics are embedded, and the second in international governance structures (Kell and Ruggie 1999).

While there has been a growth in global economic rule-making—or governance—since globalisation's impact became obvious, Kell and Ruggie argue that its main focus has been creating the 'institutional bases for the functioning of global markets', with global corporations as the key beneficiaries of the system, to the detriment of other factors such as the environment, human rights, poverty reduction and food safety. Further,

5 www.worldbank.org.

Kell and Ruggie note that large and developed nations have the means to protect themselves, while developing nations are considerably more vulnerable to the negative impacts of free market (and market-first) policies.

These shifts and imbalances have resulted in calls for a new institutional order—and international governance structure—to create a more equitable system. Kell and Ruggie argue that the UN Global Compact, which we will discuss in more detail below, was founded as one way of 'challenging the international business community to help the UN implement universal values in the areas of human rights, environment and labour' (Kell and Ruggie 1999: 3).

In the absence of mandated or regulatory frameworks that govern enterprise behaviour and practice on a global scale, the UN Global Compact is but one of many multi-sector initiatives that are attempting to create a framework of what many call 'soft law'. Soft laws are not binding or mandatory in the same way that laws issued by governments are ('hard law'), and hence cannot be enforced. But they can carry the weight of aspiration, of institutional and social pressures, and of moral persuasion that, over time and with enough reinforcement, can create changes in the world.

Indeed, many treaties and declarations issued by the UN itself can be considered soft rather than hard law, although some states have mandated elements of each; examples include, the UN Declaration on Human Rights and the Environment, the Rio Declaration, and the International Labour Organisation's conventions. Below we will explores some of these emerging—typically networked—initiatives and enterprises, starting with the Global Compact and looking at other types of boundary spanning entities, as a possible way for a new form of global governance to emerge.

The UN Global Compact: an aspirational model for global governance

In reviewing the last few hundred years, in the introduction to *Globalisation, Democracy and Terrorism*, the Marxist historian Eric Hobsbawm observed: 'The age of international empires is dead. We shall have to find another way of organising the globalised world of the 21st century—and so far we have not found it' (Hobsbawm 2007). With this statement we begin our exploration of different ways of organising our globalised world.

When UN Secretary-General Kofi Annan rose to speak at the Davos World Economic Forum on 31 January 1999, the UN Global Compact was just an idea—an aspiration—albeit with a significant provenance. By the time of its launch in New York at the UN 18 months later on 26 July 2000, it had become a set of nine principles on human rights, labour standards and environmental protection, with 42 corporate signatories. A tenth principle, on anti-corruption, was added in 2004 to aid business in its efforts to fight corruption and signal the importance of the private sector's role in doing so (see Box 1). In its first few years the Global Compact talked about 'corporate citizenship' and helping to make 'markets more stable and inclusive' (Annan 2004; 9-12).

Box 1 **UN Global Compact Principles**[6]

Human Rights

Principle 1: Support and respect the protection of international human rights within their sphere of influence.

Principle 2: Make sure their own corporations are not complicit in human rights abuses.

Labour

Principle 3: Freedom of association and the effective recognition of the right to collective bargaining.

Principle 4: The elimination of all forms of forced and compulsory labour.

Principle 5: The effective abolition of child labour.

Principle 6: The elimination of discrimination in respect of employment and occupation.

Environment

Principle 7: Support a precautionary approach to environmental challenges.

Principle 8: Undertake initiatives to promote greater environmental responsibility.

Principle 9: Encourage the development and diffusion of environmentally friendly technologies.

Anti-Corruption

Principle 10: Businesses should work against corruption in all its forms, including extortion and bribery.

---

6   www.unglobalcompact.org/AbouttheGC/TheTENPrinciples/index.html.

Yet when Kofi Annan spoke about business needing a new social compact with society, he obviously articulated something important to many observers of business. His words focused on creating 'a global compact of shared values and principles, which will give a human face to the global market' (Annan 1999: 260-61). With more than 8,000 signatories in more than 135 countries,[7] the UN Global Compact is the largest corporate citizenship initiative in the world. It now classifies itself as the 'world's only truly global political forum, as an authoritative convener and facilitator', with the capacity to bring together actors from business with those from governments, the UN itself, civil society, trade/labour unions and academia.

Fast forward ten years from its inception and the Compact is focused additionally on climate change's 'existential threat to the planet', taking on the role of enabler of 'global cooperation and partnership on a scale never seen before'. With its global reach, it could easily frame itself as 'the world's largest corporate sustainability initiative' (Ki-moon 2009) as well as the largest corporate citizenship initiative.

In the early days, both Ruggie and Kell frequently pointed out that the current (economic and social) state of affairs was not sustainable. They noted that the gap between market and community had to be closed in order to strengthen 'the fabric of global community'. Further, they argued that the values embedded in the principles of the Compact should be the rocks on which the new economy was built. With long-term vision and foresight they asked: 'Who is in control of the unpredictable forces that can bring on economic instability and social disclosure, sometimes in lightning speed?' (Ruggie 2004: 35).

Of course, from a systems perspective, there were others who knew that global economic freedom had to be matched by greater responsibility in financial and corporate markets. Ultimately, greater responsibility would mean that new global governance mechanisms, institutions and rules were needed to cope with globalisation, human security, equity and sustainability. But the science of climate change was still unclear, and many people were still getting rich from making money out of thin air. As a result, little real progress on systemic change was made until the house of cards came tumbling down at the end of 2008. Finally, more people began to see that the emperor had no clothes, no money, and had seriously damaged dwindling environmental resources.

---

7 *UN Global Compact Bulletin: August 2010*, www.unglobalcompact.org/
NewsAndEvents/UNGC_bulletin/august_2010.html, accessed 26 August 2010.

Ruggie and Kell argued in 2000, shortly after Kofi Annan's initial speech, that expanding global markets requires a social response. They contend that the significant expansion of global economic rule-making over the past decade, which basically enables global markets to function, has not been matched by comparable efforts on behalf of other global concerns, such as the environment, human rights or poverty, or, for that matter, food safety and international cartels. While the major capitalist countries have the domestic and institutional capacity to protect themselves from the worst negative effects of this imbalance, the rest of the world is far more vulnerable. As national economies have become more integrated into a global whole, Ruggie, Kell and others see a clear need for international institutions to replace the uneven patchwork of national rules and regulations. They view the Global Compact, which calls on corporations and others to work with the UN in applying environmental, labour and human rights standards, as a step in this direction' (Erb-Leoncavallo 2000).

In 1999, the UN's leadership knew that it had to embrace the reality of the economic and political process of globalisation, but there was also awareness that the going would be rough and the storms frequent. Those who promulgated the Compact were acutely aware that the UN could only catalyse, lead and promote corporate responsibility. It could lead because of the moral authority it had generated as the world's most prominent multilateral organisation representing the nations of the world. The UN, however, had no mandate to punish malfeasance, greed, fraud or dishonesty in the corporate world.

Much of the moral authority of the UN and the UN Global Compact is located within the UN Secretary-General's office. Thus, it is critically important that both Kofi Annan and his successor Ban Ki-moon have been vigorous promoters of the Compact. Successively, they have not only kept it alive, but also maintained its momentum and allowed it to grow and flourish under the UN's umbrella.

A learning and values network

From the beginning the Compact was conceived as a learning network, based on the promotion of values whose provenance lay in the enlightenment and the moral mission of the UN Charter and whose principles lay in international agreements and law. Later, Ruggie and Kell were to complain that the Compact was very much misunderstood. Too many expected too much from what was, after all, meant to be an aspirational initiative, and one quite deliberately focused on learning. It generally operates by bridging traditional sector boundaries and bringing actors from those sectors of business, government and civil society together in a learning process. Perhaps, with a system dominated by global finance and corporatism, too much was also anticipated from the Compact's systems-based learning approach to the incorporation of universal values.

The Global Compact and its networks operate in many respects (as do many of today's other new types of enterprises) as a type of viral organism. In a sense the Global Compact represents what biologist Richard Dawkins (1976) calls a 'meme'. A meme is a cultural entity that spreads much in the same way as a virus, often opportunistically, replicating itself, while evolving, mutating and adapting. New viral organisms and memes find advantage where they can, rather like the most inventive corporations and NGOs and, we argue, the Global Compact itself.

If there is one word that explains the growth of the Compact over its first ten years it is 'opportunism'. For example, where the Compact's leaders could create opportunity or ride an existing momentum, they have stepped in, using the Compact's moral mission and collaborative partnership approach to put people and organisations together that might not otherwise have met. One criticism of the Compact has been that it sometimes seems to lose focus or spread itself too thin, just as businesses sometimes do with product proliferation that dilutes a valued brand. Still, because the UN's reach is very broad, and its values foundational, the Compact's activities are unlikely to be the ones that break the proverbial camel's back (see Box 2).

Today there are many learning and associational networks that operate at a global level, and there are many CR initiatives. Few, however, have the moral authority of the UN. It is for this reason that the UN, as well as the Global Compact, has succeeded, and also for this reason that it is so attacked by some stakeholders and abused by some participants. Open societies are open to positive innovations but also to abuse, as was seen in September 2001 with the attacks on the World Trade Centre in New York. The very fabric of open markets, pluralism, democratic participation and learning networks requires neither absolutism nor fundamentalism, but tolerance. This characteristic means tolerance of digression, openness to a variety of ideas, a love of diversity, and an unshakeable adherence to the core values of the Enlightenment and the moral mission of the UN, particularly with respect to human rights and gender equality, the rule of law, and peace and security.

Box 2 **UN Charter 1945, San Francisco, USA**[8]

We the People of the United Nations, determined to save succeeding generations from the scourge of war, which twice in our lifetime has brought untold sorrow to mankind, and to reaffirm faith in fundamental human rights, in the dignity and worth of the human person, in the equal rights of men and women and of nations large and small, and to establish conditions under which justice and respect for the obligations arising from treaties and other sources of international law can be maintained, and to promote social progress and better standards of life in larger freedom, and for these ends to practice tolerance and live together in peace with one another as good neighbours, and to unite our strength to maintain international peace and security, and to ensure, by the acceptance of principles and the institution of methods, that armed force shall not be used, save in the common interest, and to employ international machinery for the promotion of the economic and social advancement of all peoples.

Beginning in 2000, the Compact established its first learning forum, a conference that brought together early signatories to share ideas about how they were approaching integration of the Compact's (then) nine principles with each other. In that first tranche of 42 companies, participants at the forum delivered 'examples of their implementation of one or more of the principles of the UN Global Compact'. Even at this stage it was clear that many of these corporate statements emanated from their public relations departments, rather than being genuine engagement or understanding of the learning basis on which the Compact was founded.

The original learning forum collapsed under the weight of external scrutiny when the companies, with a very few notable exceptions, objected to being questioned over their motives (McIntosh *et al.* 2003). Given that the idea of the Compact was to bring the market closer to the community of people, this outcome presented an obvious irony. It was also a significant problem for the Compact secretariat, which had to steer down a fast moving river with the crocodiles of capitalism on one side and the gunboats of civil society on the other. Ten years later, the advent of the 'communications on progress' has not solved the problem, with many companies being delisted every year for failing to submit their communication on

8   www.un.org/aboutun/charter.

progress. Further, some of the communications are still of dubious integrity or authenticity.[9]

Initially, the Global Compact hoped to create engagement by getting the CEOs in signatory companies to commit to the principles. Then it sought to foster learning via multi-stakeholder dialogue, global gatherings of signatories in the learning forums and through collaborative initiatives. Eventually the learning forums evolved into local and regional networks through which the Compact still operates today (Waddock 2003).

Among the issues that have been, and continue to be, raised by Compact participants regarding learning are:

- Getting chief executives to take corporate responsibility seriously;

- Ensuring a real—not just window dressing—commitment by Global Compact companies to freedom of association and collective bargaining;

- Making the business case for implementation of the Compact's principles.

Other learning includes creating multi-sector and multi-level (nations, businesses and individuals) coalitions to deal effectively with issues of corporate responsibility, engaging young people and, critically, engaging uninterested companies.[10]

Much of the Global Compact's work gets done at the local or regional level though a series of local networks established around the world. Local networks are normally, but not always, business led. They include other types of signatories as well, and serve as a focal point for interactions with the Global Compact office and other signatories. One of their primary roles is to promote multi-stakeholder engagement by including actors from other sectors in joint learning and dialogue, projects and collaborations. Further, local networks can enhance learning by supporting signatories as they develop their annual communications on progress, the main requirement for sustaining active membership in the Compact.

---

9 www.unglobalcompact.org/AbouttheGC/IntegrityMeasures/index.html, accessed 17 March 2011.

10 Global Compact Office, 'Reflections on the Global Compact's Fourth International Learning Forum Meeting', www.enewsbuilder.net/focalpoint/e_article000740358. cfm?x=b11,0,w, accessed 6 May 2009.

Progress and programmes

Over its first ten years, the Global Compact held additional learning forums in Berlin (2002), Brazil (2003) and Ghana (2006). There have been two International Global Compact Leaders Summits, the first in New York in 2004 and the second in Geneva in 2007. A third marked the tenth anniversary in New York in July 2010. At the 2004 summit, the then UN Secretary-General Kofi Annan announced the adoption of the tenth Global Compact principle 'against corruption in all its forms, including corruption and bribery'. Further, 20 major investment companies endorsed a Global Compact report 'connecting financial markets to environmental, social and governance criteria', agreeing to take further initiatives to ensure that such ESG criteria would be embedded in both financial and corporate decision-making. Representing some US$6 trillion in total assets, these companies ultimately launched, in partnership with the Global Compact and the UN Environmental Programme (UNEP), what have become the Principles for Responsible Investment.[11] Other initiatives were the Growing Sustainable Business Initiative, launched by the United Nations Development Programme (UNDP).[12]

At the Global Compact Summit in Shanghai, China in 2005, participants adopted the Shanghai Declaration. Among the agreements in the Shanghai Declaration were: 'We, the participants of the UN Global Compact Summit: China, commit to continuously advance the implementation of the UN Global Compact and its Principles. We will strive to give concrete meaning to a principle-based approach in our operations.'[13]

The Leaders Summit, held in Geneva in 2007, generated two important initiatives. First was the Geneva Declaration, a 21-point document that spells out specific actions that businesses, governments and Global Compact participants can engage in.[14] The Geneva Declaration is based on the premise that 'business, as a key agent of globalisation, can be an enormous force for good', and that: 'Globalisation, if rooted in universal principles,

---

11 www.unpri.org, accessed 12 May 2009.
12 www.undp.org/partners/business/gsb/index.shtml, accessed 12 May 2009.
13 'Final Report of the Global Compact Summit: China', unglobalcompact.org/docs/ news_events/8.1/China_Summit_Final_Report.pdf: 31, accessed 12 May 2009.
14 unglobalcompact.org/NewsAndEvents/event_archives/Leaders_Summit_2007. html, accessed 12 May 2009.

has the power to improve our world fundamentally—delivering economic and social benefits to people, communities, and markets everywhere.'[15]

At the same Summit, the Principles for Responsible Management Education were introduced and adopted.[16] In addition, a Summary of Ministerial Roundtable on the Role of Governments in Promoting Responsible Corporate Citizenship was adopted by government ministers, and executives of 150 companies pledged to speed up action on climate change through the Caring for Climate platform, asking governments for action beyond the Kyoto Protocol. Among numerous other initiatives, the CEO Water Mandate was also introduced.[17]

In 2008, the African Private Sector Forum was held in Addis Ababa, Ethiopia, with the objectives of assessing Africa's industrial development potential, highlighting the importance of good corporate governance and citizenship, examining the role of the private sector in contributing to sustainable development and promoting public–private partnerships.[18] Also in 2008, the Compact co-organised with UNDP, the Office of the Coordinator for Humanitarian Affairs, the UN Department for Economic and Social Affairs, and the UN Office for Partnerships a first-ever private sector forum. This forum brought together about 100 chief executives from different parts of the world, governmental heads of state, civil society leaders, foundation heads and UN agency heads to discuss how to move the Millennium Development Goals forward.[19] Further, in 2008, the first meeting of the Caring for Climate Signatories was held in Geneva, jointly organised with the Global Compact, UNEP and the World Business Council for Sustainable Development.[20] In addition, a Leading US Companies Retreat was held for multinational corporations in collaboration with AccountAbility and the Boston College Centre for Corporate Citizenship. This group

---

15 'The Geneva Declaration', unglobalcompact.org/docs/summit2007/GENEVA_DECLARATION.pdf, accessed 12 May 2009.

16 www.unprme.org, accessed 19 March 2010.

17 unglobalcompact.org/docs/news_events/8.1/GC_Summit_Report_07.pdf, accessed 12 May 2009.

18 unglobalcompact.org/NewsAndEvents/event_archives/2008_AU_summit/index.html, accessed 12 May 2009.

19 unglobalcompact.org/NewsAndEvents/event_archives/2008_UN_Private_Sector_Forum/index.html, accessed 12 May 2009.

20 unglobalcompact.org/Issues/Environment/Climate_Change/meeting_of_signatories.html, accessed 12 May 2009.

of companies became the GCLead, a corporate leadership group of Global Compact signatories in 2009.[21]

At the June 2010 International Leaders Summit held at UN Headquarters in New York, the leaders adopted the New York Declaration by Business, outlining business's commitment to the Global Compact and calling for an embedding of the ten principles into corporate strategies and operations. The Blueprint for Corporate Sustainability Leadership was also launched. In addition, two new initiatives, the Women's Empowerment Principles and the Principles for Social Investment, were introduced, and a wide range of new resources for integrating the UNGC principles were also launched.[22]

Clearly, from this brief list of some of the more prominent activities of the Global Compact, there has been significant activity and movement to bring together actors from different sectors around the Compact's set of principles. As of early 2010, the Global Compact's signatories included 5,200 businesses, spanning across sector boundaries to include governments, labour organisations, CSOs and NGOs, and several UN agencies.

Boundary spanning

The shifting context that exists today places many demands on executives in all types of enterprise to cross boundaries. The US-based Centre for Creative Leadership (CCL) undertook a survey of CEOs in 2009 to determine what their perspectives on 'boundary spanning leadership' were. Defining boundary spanning leadership, 'as the capability to establish direction, alignment and commitment across boundaries in service of a higher vision or goal' (Ernst and Yip 2009), the Centre surveyed 128 top executives about their boundary spanning activities and perspectives. As we do, the CCL reasoned that the complexity of negotiating boundaries means that very different types of leadership will be needed in the future. Important skills are 'the capability to create direction, alignment and commitment across boundaries in service of a higher vision or goal' (Yip, Ernst and Campbell 2009: 4).

21 www.unglobalcompact.org/docs/news_events/8.1/UNGC-Leading_Companies_ Retreat_Summary_Report.pdf, accessed 12 May 2009.
22 www.unglobalcompact.org/AboutTheGC/tools_resources/leaders_summit_2010. html, accessed 17 March 2011.

Almost all of the leaders interviewed noted the importance of working across boundaries, although only slightly more than half thought that their peers were effective in doing so, and they believed that fewer than 20% of middle managers had this capability (Yip, Ernst and Campbell 2009). The criticality of boundary spanning, in the eyes of these leaders, arose from the need for innovation which, as we have seen in previous chapters, is occurring across rather than within traditional boundaries, forcing executives to step outside their comfort zones.

The CCL's study defined several types of 'mission critical' boundaries that executives need to span—vertical or across levels and hierarchy within enterprises; horizontal or across functional expertise; stakeholder boundaries which are beyond the firm's own boundaries (i.e. related to CR initiatives as discussed earlier); demographic (because the business world has globalised, which means that gender, ethnic, cultural and national boundaries are constantly being crossed); and geographic. The most frequent boundary that executives felt needed crossing was horizontal (within the firm); however, geographic, demographic and stakeholder boundaries also received particular mention, especially within the realm of top executives (Yip, Ernst and Campbell 2009: 14).

The trends uncovered by the CCL are exacerbated by what we have called SEE Change, which demands that executives at many levels of enterprise be able to cope effectively with the demands and issues coming from partners and collaborators, alliances and stakeholders in domains different from their own. Joining initiatives such as the UN Global Compact or multi-stakeholder forums place business and other leaders in entirely new contexts in which they are interacting with others from very different geographical areas and spheres of activity, and with widely different cultural and business perspectives. Even leaders from smaller enterprises, such as those described in Chapter 6, face increased complexity by the very reality that the innovations they are developing inherently cross multiple boundaries. And when leaders recognise the complexity of the issues facing the world and their businesses, they increasingly join other types of boundary spanning initiatives, such as the ones discussed below.

Global action networks

One interesting new type of network enterprise that has emerged in the context of the internet is the GAN (global action network).[23] GANs take the network concept even further than the extended enterprises discussed in earlier chapters. As communications technology has allowed the cloud of information and connectivity to develop, so too does it allow for people in far flung places to connect, work across distances and accomplish common objectives with each other that might once have been unthinkable. As the CCL report discussed, such entities can sometimes develop higher level goals that they attempt to achieve together (Yip, Ernst and Campbell 2009). GANs generally are global in scope, focus on issues of the common good or public interest, use an interdisciplinary approach based in action-learning to experiment around challenges that have seemed intractable in the past. They operate by bringing together a diverse network of stakeholders oriented towards creating systems change. Box 3 summarises the major characteristics of a GAN.

Box 3 **Definition of global action network**[24]

GANs are a specific type of innovation that brings together five strategic qualities. A GAN's strategy:

- Is global.
- Focuses on issues of common public interest (not profit-seeking).
- Develops interdisciplinary action-learning with real-time experiments to address novel and enduring challenges.
- Creates a diverse network of organisations of stakeholders.
- Generates systemic change by creating cross-sectoral (business–government–civil society) actions.

Implicitly, and sometimes explicitly, GANs create an emergent set of pressures on participants, as well as others in the participants' industries, which attempt to move the industry, business practice or systems towards their goals. Although there are no enforcement mechanisms in

---

23 GAN is a construct jointly developed by Steve Waddell and Rajeev Khagram. More information can be found at www.scalingimpact.net/?p=gan, accessed 27 April 2009. See also Waddell 2010.

24 www.scalingimpact.net/?p=gan.

many GANs, they do represent a form of soft law because they typically attempt to establish standards of practice that improve a given situation, much as the Global Compact, which can be classified as a GAN, has done with respect to CR. Some GANs, however, do develop 'marking' or standard-setting practices that create new industry norms and standards with a degree of reputational sanctioning impact.

In addition to the Global Compact, another well-known example of a GAN in the CR arena is the Global Reporting Initiative (GRI). In a relatively short period of time, the GRI has become the global standard for ESG (beyond financial or multiple-bottom-line) reporting. According to its co-founder Allen White, without the technological connectivity of the internet, it would have taken years to develop (if, indeed, it could have been developed at all) (Waddock 2008b).

The GRI was founded by two individuals with the backing of the environmental organisation Ceres, and then developed through a global multi-stakeholder coalition with different interests in the emergence of an ESG reporting framework. Notwithstanding the widely differing perspectives of the participating individuals and representatives of organisations, ultimately they were able to find common ground under what co-founder Allen White calls a 'big tent'. They could accomplish this ongoing task because they could readily and virtually instantly communicate, make changes to the framework and build agreement about key components online (Brown, de Jong and Lessidrenska 2007).

The GRI is a GAN because it crosses numerous boundaries, including geographical, political and sector. According to Sanjeev Khagram and Steve Waddell, GANs are truly global and multi-level in structure, focused on implementing interdisciplinary action learning and reflective action. They build stable and flexible multi-stakeholder, cross-sectoral and inter-organisational networks to accomplish their work of generating system change.

The work of GANs, which can be found in multiple industries and all sectors, is fundamentally about achieving the public good, largely through non-governmental means that involve boundary spanning and creating an enterprise in which diversity thrives.[25] Interestingly, GANs tend not to include governmental actors (although occasionally they do), despite the fact that many of them deal with issues relating to the common good or public interest. In addition to the GRI and the Global Compact, examples of GANs include: Forest Stewardship Council; Global Water Partnership;

25 www.scalingimpact.net/gan/global-action-network.

Marine Stewardship Council; Transparency International; Micro-credit Summit Campaign; and Youth Employment Systems. GANs thus typically operate in a relevant public policy sphere, creating an emergent form of global governance through a type of peer group pressure and 'soft' enforcement tactics.

Inherently collaborative by nature, GANs gain their legitimacy by involving numerous actors (stakeholders) and providing them with a sense of 'voice' or input into decision-making processes. Although GANs do not have the typical coercive powers and formal authority associated with governmental entities, their work carries a certain legitimacy and moral persuasiveness because they typically focus on public policy issues in the 'public interest' by involving members of the relevant public interest groups. GANs, by their nature, engage with a wide swath of interested stakeholders, and thus can claim a degree of representativeness and inclusiveness. Because they, and whatever actions they take are voluntary, however, GANs need to rely on the power of persuasion and peer pressure, association and relationships to generate and enforce standards (when relevant) rather than traditional enforcement mechanisms to accomplish their purposes.

In one sense, GANs are archetypal of SEE Change organisations because they are inherently more networked, boundary spanning and democratic than traditional organisations. In addition, many of them emphasise social or environmental goals, even when they are supporting the work of industries or companies (e.g. the Forest Stewardship Council or the UN Global Compact). In another sense, because they sometimes do not engage governmental bodies, they can raise questions about whether the public interest is actually being served or not. And, as the CCL study indicates, they inherently pose greater degrees of complexity and boundary spanning for leaders.

Civil society and non-governmental organisations and enterprises

Ecologist Paul Hawken has written extensively about another type of enterprise that is seeking to change the world in positive ways. 'Blessed unrest' enterprises are based in civil society and can consist of anything from an individual working for positive change to a global organisation

(Hawken 2008). Hawken estimates that there are, perhaps, as many as two million blessed unrest enterprises making up the largest social movement the world has known.

Bornstein agrees that there are many NGOs, CSOs and citizen sector enterprises in the world today. He reports more than 2,000 environmental organisations in Indonesia alone, and 20,000 economic development NGOs in Bangladesh. And he points out that Brazil registered 400,000 citizen enterprises in the 1990s, while the US saw a 60% increase to more than 700,000, with estimates for the total as high as a million in Brazil and two million in the US (Bornstein 2007: 4). Clearly, this sector has burgeoned in recent years.

Blessed unrest, according to Hawken, is a movement unlike any other. It is without a name, without a clear leader and without a centre. Yet its enterprises share a focus on the achievement of social justice and ecological sustainability. CSOs or NGOs work towards a huge variety of progressive causes broadly associated with these goals.

As Hawken has noted, CSOs and NGOs have proliferated rapidly during and since the late 20th century. This growth occurred because the role of government changed, becoming weaker in the face of the global power of corporations. After World War II there was less deference to established authority in countries with developed democracies. Stakeholder empowerment, as witnessed by the growth of CSOs and NGOs, is a response to that shift. These enterprises, like GANs, provide a form of countervailing power that represents not just the economic interests of business or the territorial and coercive interests of states, but also the human interests of societies and civilisation. CSOs, NGOs and citizen sector enterprises can be very small or quite large, can focus narrowly on a small issue or be global in scope. Collectively, they represent a wide range of interests, including environmental protection and nature conservation, trade union rights, working conditions, human rights, poverty, water, energy and the interests of specific groups, to name but a few. They span both secular and religious interests, as well as encompassing the entire political spectrum.

Multi-stakeholder dialogue

Another type of SEE Change enterprise, perhaps not so new but certainly buoyed up by the connectivity of electronic devices, is that of associations, gatherings and other types of convening that are focused around a combination of dialogue and action. Since the late 1990s, these associations have increasingly taken the form of multi-stakeholder engagements. Implicitly or explicitly they recognise what management theorist Russell Ackoff (1975) called 'messes'. Messes are intractable complex problems that can only be solved by involving actors from all of the sectors affected by the mess or complex issue. Associational activities include traditional conferences and dialogue groups, as well as multi-stakeholder gatherings that use either traditional conventions or more engaging approaches to bring people together, such as future search conferencing, open space or world café formats. These gatherings come together so that participants can get to know each other, learn, engage in developing new understanding and knowledge, and develop action plans collectively.

More and more, however, such gatherings attempt to go beyond interaction and dialogue to focus on action outcomes. Multi-stakeholder dialogues sometimes focus on problem-solving or building consensus, goals that are inherently more complex and difficult to achieve than simply building relationships, sharing information or setting agendas (Susskind *et al.* 2003). The idea behind bringing multiple stakeholders into dialogue is to 'get the whole system into the room' so that all those stakeholders affected by the issue at hand can have a say in its potential resolution (Senge 1990).

Techniques such as open space technology, world café formats, mind-mapping and appreciative inquiry bring together multiple stakeholders with different perspectives to focus on shared problems. These encounters frequently focus on developing mutual or collaborative action projects that explicitly cross sector and organisational boundaries. The understanding that underlies these initiatives is that many of today's problems are too complex to be resolved by single entities, or even by multiple entities of a single type, so crossing boundaries and gaining new perspectives is essential to designing the new solutions that are needed.

The UN Global Compact and the GRI have both generated action-oriented stakeholder-engaged dialogue as a way of moving from ideas to action. Similarly, the WBCSD (World Business Council for Sustainable Development) brings together multiple stakeholders from the business community to promote progressive ideas about sustainability, while EABIS (The Academy for Business in Society)[26] brings together companies, business schools, academic institutions and the European Commission as a way of integrating business in society issues into the heart of

26 www.eabis.org/about/about-eabis-5.html, accessed 20 May 2009.

both theory and practice of business in Europe. APABIS, the Asia-Pacific Academy of Business in Society, a recently formed network, plays a similar role in its region.[27]

Cross-/multi-sector collaborations/ partnerships

For years, some multinational companies have been engaging with civil society and governmental sectors through social, cross-sector or public–private partnerships and collaborations. Like the multi-stakeholder gatherings discussed above, these initiatives tackle social and ecological problems that tend to cross boundaries. However, they tend to be problem-focused with specific collaboratively based or developed strategies. Unlike a multi-stakeholder gathering, which disbands once its time-frame is completed, collaborations and partnerships take a permanent or semi-permanent form with an action agenda. Often (although not always), these collaborations develop an organisational structure that draws resources of various kinds from different partners. They can develop ongoing purposes, strategies and goals, complete with budget and dedicated staff.

These collaborations can focus on anything from standard-setting and implementation across-the-board in an industry to specific initiatives that deal with particular issues in local areas. For example, many companies join in public–private partnerships with local schools in an effort to improve educational delivery and ensure that graduates are ready for the reality of work. Other collaborations deal with issues such as water resources, job training, obesity or HIV/AIDS.

Going forward in a networked world

The world of networked enterprises that we have explored in this chapter is changing the way we view enterprises, what it means to develop a sustainable enterprise economy and how to lead in this emerging context. These subjects will be the topics of the final chapters.

---

27 www.apabis.org, accessed 19 February 2010.

8
Towards sustainable enterprise

Moving to SEE:
sustainable . . . enterprise . . . economy

As we have seen, SEE Change enterprises can be focused or have mixed purposes, be large or very small, operate independently and be linked to similar enterprises or to very different ones; and they can be for-profit, not-for-profit, networks, NGOs or boundary spanners. These 'businesses unusual' can be big businesses, even large corporations, or small and medium-sized enterprises, private or public. Frequently they merge profitability with social goals, crossing boundaries that used to be reserved for public or private or governmental institutions. Considered as a phenomenon, particularly in light of the financial meltdown and now apparent flaws in the previous models of enterprise and competitive strategy, SEE Change enterprises may well represent the type of sea change—and hope—that can potentially bring about a move towards sustainability, social justice and human dignity. These attributes have been lacking in older models of capitalism which are focused more narrowly on maximisation of shareholder wealth.

SEE Change *is* capitalism—but it is capitalism with a human face, a more Earth-centric orientation and a more explicitly social agenda. We are already seeing that current economic and environmental crises are creating new ideas and new organisational innovations. New ways of thinking are desperately needed if humankind is to thrive in the future. In this chapter, we will explore SEE Change organisations as hopeful signs of the type and direction of change needed.

The sustainable enterprise economy

Enterprises of SEE Change are vibrant, flexible, values-driven and grounded in a realistic relationship to natural systems. The sustainable human-scale corporation is founded on specific conditions: low ecological footprint; enhanced social equity; and an extended sense of futurity. Sustainable enterprise is therefore characterised by long-term life and appropriate size (rather than immortality and unlimited size), as well as a balance of power among, and accountability to, a range of relevant stakeholders.

The sustainable enterprise *economy* (SEE), as we see it, is an economy that sees no necessary conflict between self-interest and obligation to community, where any enterprise—corporate, social, public, state-owned or individual—aims to have as little impact on the environment as possible *and* is mindful of its social impact. In an enterprise economy, the spirit of the community is geared to risk-taking, innovation, creativity, problem-solving, entrepreneurialism and enthusiasm for life, but also recognises that mobility, exchange and trade are part of what it means to be human. A *sustainable* enterprise economy uses these human characteristics to create wealth and nurture wellbeing within a framework of peace and social justice that includes equitable income distribution based not simply on already aggregated power and influence, but also on genuine inputs and outcomes that benefit society. Furthermore, it is premised on the provision of fundamental public 'goods', such as health and education, the observance of the rule of law and the upholding of human rights. SEE preserves natural capital, but it also creates social and human capital at the same time.

SEE builds on the idea of 'natural capital', a concept pioneered by Paul Hawken, Amory Lovins and Hunter Lovins (1999). Their book, *Natural Capitalism*, argues that four major shifts are needed to better align human society with nature's resources. First, they argue that we need to dramatically increase the productivity of natural resources and reduce the waste inherent in the system, a message that the innovative online video 'The Story of Stuff' vividly illustrates.[1] Second, they argue for a shift to more ecologically centric or biologically inspired production models where there is no waste (because what is waste for one system becomes a resource for others). Of course, such approaches mean eliminating many of the toxins and hazardous substances inherent in today's production systems and products. Third, they argue for a solutions-based business model that redefines wellbeing to encompass satisfaction with quality, usefulness and performance, not just the acquisition of ever more goods or services. Fourth, they make the point that there needs to be a significant reinvestment in natural capital itself—restoring the planet's ecological systems so that they can continue to support life.

Another book, released in 2002 and updated in 2004 (Cavanagh *et al.* 2002), argues for building the economy not on free trade and market liberalisation, but rather on an entirely different set of principles focused on equity, sustainability and diversity. The authors discuss the principle of 'living democracy' which advocates building regional and international institutions that are democratic and accountable, while supporting community and national sovereignty. These principles are bolstered by the concept of subsidiarity, which means favouring the local (or regional) over the global in policy decisions, and the concept of ecological sustainability including biodiversity and environmental protection. The authors also argue for valuing diversity (cultural, ethnic, religious and economic) as a basis of resilience and vitality that provides for innovation capacity, human rights, provision of jobs and livelihoods, equity and social justice.

All of these principles rest on the so-called 'precautionary principle' which was prominently articulated at the 1992 Earth Summit which resulted in the Rio Declaration. The Rio Declaration's Principle 15 states:[2]

> In order to protect the environment, the precautionary approach shall be widely applied by states according to their capabilities. Where there are threats of serious or irreversible damage, lack of full scientific certainty shall not be used as a reason for postponing cost-effective measures to prevent environmental degradation.

SEE is obviously for business, but it is also inclusive of other types of enterprises and organisations, as we have demonstrated in the past few

1 www.storyofstuff.com.
2 www.unep.org/Documents.multilingual/Default.asp?DocumentID=78&ArticleID =1163, accessed 6 January 2010.

chapters. The challenge is for all institutions to change the way they relate to local and global environmental and social issues. This means government departments rethinking the way they work, community organisations and local government reorganising themselves, global corporations aligning their mission, purpose and practices with the realities of climate change and sustainable development, and individuals actively participating in the change. We will explore these changes and what is needed to accomplish them in more detail below, focusing at a higher level of abstraction than in previous chapters. Boxes 1 and 2 highlight some examples of change initiatives that are already under way.

Box 1 **Slow Food, slow movement**[3]

The Slow Food Movement aims 'to counteract fast food and fast life, the disappearance of local food traditions and people's dwindling interest in the food they eat, where it comes from, how it tastes and how our food choices affect the rest of the world'. Slow food inherently takes into account the way that food is produced, its nutritional and gastronomic benefits, and sustainability issues—both for producers and for the natural environment. The Slow Food Movement internationalised in 1989 when representatives of 15 nations endorsed a 'slow food' manifesto that, among other things, claims that: 'We are enslaved by speed and have all succumbed to the same insidious virus: Fast Life, which disrupts our habits, pervades the privacy of our homes and forces us to eat Fast Foods.' The Slow Food manifesto argues for rediscovering local flavours, preserving culture by 'developing taste rather than demeaning it', and 'guarantee[ing] a better future'.

From modest beginnings, the Slow Food Movement now claims more than 100,000 members in 132 countries working to defend biodiversity in the food supply, educate people about the enjoyment of good food, and produce food in responsible ways. Slow Food is part of a broader movement to slow the world's ever escalating pace—the 'Slow Movement'.[4] The Slow Movement focuses on the issue of 'time poverty' by findings ways to slow travel, cities, food, schools, books, living and money in an ever-expanding set of slow downs. The Slow Movement operates by helping people make connections to each other, to place, to food—essentially to what is meaningful in life—rather than simply continuing on the treadmill that is modern living.

3 www.slowfood.com.
4 www.slowmovement.com.

Box 2 **Business Alliance for Local Living Economies**[5]

BALLE, the Business Alliance for Local Living Economies, is an effort to change the current globalisation project by strengthening the efforts of entrepreneurs in the US and Canada to flourish locally while remaining ecologically responsible and accountable to key stakeholders. At the time of writing BALLE had 80 community-based networks of local businesses with more than 21,000 independent businesses. BALLE's mission is to 'catalyse, strengthen and connect networks of locally owned independent businesses dedicated to building strong Local Living Economies'. BALLE helps local businesses collaborate on a vision of cities and towns engaged in 'shared learning, sustainable agriculture, green building, renewable energy, community capital, zero-waste manufacturing and independent retail'. BALLE's belief is that these are the fundamentals—the building blocks—for successful locally based economies that are healthy, forward-looking and sustainable.

The sustainable economy enterprise

The array of enterprises that have been broadly defined as part of the sustainable enterprise economy suggests that SEE Change is an emergent phenomenon that is evolving simultaneously in many different ways (and not necessarily in a linear fashion), with many different types of entities. SEE Change is part of a process of system change that, like all complex systems, is inherently chaotic. In chaotic systems it is possible to foresee patterns and general trends, even while the specifics of a given situation (enterprise) may not be predictable. So it is with the emergence of a sustainable enterprise economy, which comes in fits and starts, with initiatives here and there, and many variations, some of which will succeed and others which will not.

A sustainable enterprise economy is fundamentally about how we grow peace, security, social justice and enterprise simultaneously; and how we cope with the pressures of population shifts and growth, limited resources and significant equity and resource distribution problems in the future. Fundamentally, it is about making a choice to build a better world for our

5 www.livingeconomies.org.

children's children rather than continuing along a path littered with inequity, lack of ecological sustainability and economic devastation.

Like the numerous entities that Paul Hawken (2008) argues comprise 'blessed unrest', SEE Change enterprises, while vastly different in form, scope and purpose, do share commonalities. Some of what we discuss below may seem obvious; and some might be radical or system changing. We hope that both perspectives are true, and that these ideas help others build forward-looking enterprises that can cope with the manifold problems facing the world today. We can only build a positive future based on what we know, and what we know how to do. One thing we do know is that the current system desperately needs reshaping if it is to provide for future generations' wellbeing.

As we see it, the emerging SEE is based on the core principles that speak to our highest sense of humanity; and on values that go well beyond profit maximising. Indeed, it is built on hopeful myths and stories that create meaning on a human scale. And it is focused on the long-term health of future generations and planet Earth itself. These ideas will be used to build a case for major systems change to bring about the sea change that will be needed for us to really see change for the better.

We believe that SEE Change enterprises have:

- Principles and values;

- Purpose;

- Meaning;

- Blended values;

- Authenticity and integrity;

- Human-scale.

We unpack each of these elements below

Principle- and values-based

The principles on which SEE Change enterprises are based go well beyond those associated with shareholder primacy and maximisation of shareholder wealth. Most businesses claim to be based on a set of principles or values. The key, of course, is whether they actually live up to those principles in their actions.

Relevant principles for SEE Change tend to be progressive and aspirational, as is evidenced in the principles underlying the UN Global

Compact, or the accountability and transparency principles of the GRI. In addition, principles are often derived from globally agreed documents that attempt to establish a sense of universality because they are widely agreed—but that have yet to be fully put into practice globally. In that sense, these principles tend to be aspirational, focused on the best of what humanity can and might be willing to do. The principles are very much aligned with principles and values like the ones at the core of the UN Global Compact around human and labour rights, ecological sustainability and a corruption-free world that puts the welfare of people, societies and the planet ahead of finances.

In addition to traditional codes of conduct and standards of practice, SEE Change enterprises emphasise foundational principles associated with basic human dignity, ecological sustainability and social justice. Such principles and values are the closest humanity has come to universal ethical standards, what have been termed 'hypernorms' (Donaldson and Dunfee 1999). The principles of the UN Global Compact are among the world's best known set of principles applied directly to enterprise (and, of course, nation states since they are drawn from globally agreed treaties). Such principles will, we believe, need to be threaded through the sustainable enterprise economy and within the enterprises that comprise it. Along with specific codes of conduct that apply to various industries and organisations, the more general principles of the UN Global Compact help guide the strategies and production practices of SEE enterprises.

Let us take the first principle of the UN Global Compact as an example: 'Business should support and respect the protection of internationally proclaimed human rights.' Like all of the Global Compact's principles, it is based on globally agreed documents, in this case Article 1 of the UN Declaration on Human Rights:

> All human beings are born free and equal in dignity and rights. They are endowed with reason and conscience and should act towards one another in a spirit of brotherhood.

This principle of human dignity is in accord with the Global Compact's second principle which requires signatories not to be complicit in human rights abuses. It is also consistent with Donaldson and Dunfee's hypernorms (1999), of which human dignity is at the core. Of course, merely stating that principles—or human rights in this case—are important, and that an enterprise will uphold them, does not ensure that reality matches rhetoric. Nevertheless, the Global Compact's ten principles provide an aspirational framework of core values based on global agreements.

Following these principles sets an ethical floor or baseline set of standards that can, if implemented broadly, raise the expectation that all types of enterprises in the future will conform to basic norms established by multilateral entities such as the UN. Such agreed principles can potentially form a foundation for a humanised global governance framework.

The Global Compact's 'aspirations' are quite simple and fundamental—that people treat each other, and the planet, with respect and dignity. That includes respecting human rights, workers rights, the natural environment and the integrity of society, all of which are articulated in the Global Compact's ten principles. Nothing, we believe, could be more fundamental to 'humanising' enterprise than these basic principles.

Mission- or purpose-driven

When they are for-profit enterprises, SEE Change enterprises emphasise goals that go well beyond profitability to include social and ecological benefits and generating wealth for all stakeholders affected by their activities, not just shareholders (Freeman 1984; Freeman, Harrison and Wicks 2007). Like the enterprises created by social entrepreneurs and for-benefit corporations, discussed earlier, they are likely to do this in a blended value way. Other types of enterprises are also mission-driven, frequently with specific social purpose goals that, to the creators of the enterprise, serve a public interest or common good purpose.

Purpose is something that helps to create meaning within enterprises, but that purpose has to be something more than simply making a profit or attempting to 'maximise shareholder wealth'. Most people, we believe, are seeking meaning in their work. When an enterprise's purpose is clearly articulated—and its contribution to the world around it is evident—then it becomes possible for people to define their work as meaningful. For most, the goal of maximising shareholder wealth does not hold much inherent purpose beyond material acquisition, while broader goals that serve the world, people or human need in some way can provide such purpose (see Box 3). Thus, Southwest Airlines identifies its purpose as 'democratising the skies' and the US's Whole Foods vision (see Box 3, Chapter 5) reaches to 'whole food, whole people, whole planet'. Such purposes take what might seem mundane—air travel and retail food sales—and articulate what the underlying or fundamental purpose is in ways that employees, customers, investors and other stakeholders can identify with.

Box 3 **Equal Exchange**[6]

Equal Exchange is a company identified by *Fast Company* magazine as one of 45 social entrepreneurial ventures that are changing the world.[7] Based on the principle of fair trade—that producers should receive fair compensation for their efforts—Equal Exchange has been, as the company itself claims, creating 'Big Change' since its founding in 1986, by selling coffee, tea and chocolate drink products from small farmers in Africa, Asia, Latin America and the United States. Working from its foundational principles, the 100% employee-owned cooperative was a pioneer in fair trade, helping to introduce fair trade coffee in mainstream US markets, following the principles of open-book management, and developing ambitious long-term objectives around a more just and sustainable world.

Equal Exchange articulates its founding principles in its mission statement. The mission is: '. . . to build long-term trade partnerships that are economically just and environmentally sound, to foster mutually beneficial relationships between farmers and consumers, and to demonstrate, through our success, the contribution of worker cooperatives and fair trade to a more equitable, democratic and sustainable world'. As with other social entrepreneurial ventures, Equal Exchange's principles led directly to a vision that provides a core of meaning around its work. Its vision, as stated on the company's website is that 'There will be . . . a vibrant mutually cooperative community of two million committed participants trading fairly one billion dollars a year in a way that transforms the world.'

Although achieving this vision is still in the future, Equal Exchange has already made a difference in many farmers' lives and, along the way, averaged 30% annual revenue growth. It now has revenues of around US$28 million per year.

Meaningfulness

One key gap in many peoples' lives these days is a sense of the meaningfulness of either their own work or that of the enterprise as a whole. SEE Change enterprises, because they are purpose-driven and quite explicit about their purposes, are likely to provide an antidote to the

---

6 www.equalexchange.coop.
7 Fast Company, '45 Social Entrepreneurs Who Are Changing the World: Equal Exchange', www.fastcompany.com/social/2008/profiles/equal-exchange.html, accessed 23 February 2010.

meaningfulness vacuum that exists in many of today's enterprises. A series of Roundtables on Sustainable Enterprise that McIntosh organised around the globe uncovered a deep hunger among many participants for more meaningful enterprises. Since work takes up a large part of most people's lives, frequently they can begin to find some meaning when they can clearly see how their enterprise is contributing to society, humanity or improving the natural environment. In this context, the communication of the message is an important element in constructing the meaning of an enterprise in such a way that key stakeholders are attracted to it, enabling them to sustain a relationship with it over long periods of time.

For some enterprises the issue of sustainability has become a lens through which meaning can be focused. For others, meaning is found in the multiple purposes defined by the blended value approach, which combines pro-social or pro-ecological goals with more traditional ones, and creates a context in which meaning and connection can more readily be generated than simply with financial goals.

Blended value

SEE Change enterprises are also starting to master what Jed Emerson (2003) has called 'blended value'. The blended value proposition, according to Emerson, is that all enterprises, no matter what their specific type or emphasis, create not just economic *or* social value, but a combination of economic, social *and* ecological value. Unlike some who would separate the values basis of companies and other types of enterprise from their value (-adding) components, the blended value proposition suggest that all three forms of capital are simultaneously created. Stakeholder theorist R. Edward Freeman has similarly argued that separating ethics from management practice represents what he terms the 'separation thesis'. Freeman argues that, in fact, ethics, values and organisational performance are integrally related and cannot be separated (Freeman, Harrison and Wicks 2007). Waddock (2009) has argued that stakeholder and ecological responsibilities are inextricably embedded in corporate strategies and practices.

Effectively, this necessary integration means that sustainable economy enterprises explicitly integrate multiple bottom lines, rather than pretending that impacts in social and ecological areas do not exist from business practices or simply attempting to externalise such costs. As we have already seen, something quite similar is happening with the blurring of sector and organisational boundaries. These multiple-bottom-line orientations will be deeply interwoven with the enterprise's core purposes in SEE Change enterprises (see Box 4). The multiple-bottom-line mission also creates an enterprise context in which the meaning of the work being done is deeply embedded and provides a holistic framework that can help to link employees and other stakeholders to the enterprise. Such ties are not just monetary but related to the mission.

Box 4 **New Leaf Paper**[8]

A company recognised by *Fast Company* for its multiple-bottom-line (blended value) orientation and sense of purpose is New Leaf Paper, which is the leading player in the paper industry for environmentally friendly printing and office supplies. Each of its 30 plus uncoated, coated and board grade papers is designed to demonstrate 'to [its] customers and the paper industry that using environmentally sound paper is an economical as well as responsible choice'. With a mission to 'be the leading national source for environmentally responsible, economically sound paper' that also meets customer needs and 'to inspire—through [its] success—a fundamental shift toward environmental responsibility in the paper industry', New Leaf Paper claims to have saved nearly 1.7 million trees, 473 million gallons of water, 897,000 million Btus of energy, 81 million pounds of solid waste and 143 million pounds of greenhouse gases by using post-consumer waste fibre rather than virgin fibre between 1998 and 2008.[9]

New Leaf Paper has accomplished these feats in an industry commonly regarded as one of the world's worst environmental performers. Its mission focuses directly on changing the industry through demonstrating its own success using more eco-friendly practices. Furthermore, the company is unafraid to compare its papers to others in the industry, 'unconditionally guarantee[ing its] papers to measure up to the quality standards of comparable, less environmentally sound papers'.

Integrity and authenticity create alignment with purpose

Voices throughout the world are calling for enterprises that are founded on integrity and clear values in a post-modern world of spin, anything goes and market driven values. They seek calm, purposeful, collaborative and responsible management approaches, rather than management

8 www.newleafpaper.com/about.html, accessed 23 February 2010.
9 eco.newleafpaper.com/audits/new, accessed 23 February 2010.

styles geared at amassing more power and focused solely on growth. That is, they seek enterprises with integrity and authenticity. Integrity means wholeness, acknowledging the whole system in which an enterprise exists and the connectedness of all the parts to each other. Integrity also means honesty and forthrightness, so that what is communicated internally and externally is aligned with the broader purposes articulated by the enterprise.

More important, however, than communicating the message of the enterprise effectively is ensuring that the strategies and practices developed by the enterprise to implement its purposes are authentic—and that stakeholders, whether employees, customers, investors, suppliers and others, can see consistency between message and practice. In their ground-breaking book *Built to Last*, James Collins and Gerry Porras (1997) found that highly successful companies tended to have clearly articulated, meaningful 'visions' that they consistently strived to live up to, so creating integrity. This work was later complemented by Collins' book on leadership, *Good to Great*, which identified how successful companies integrate an authentic vision into their business practices (Collins 2001).

Too many modern companies, however, articulate a lofty set of values, for example, about the importance of their employees, but then proceed to mass redundancies as part of retrenchment strategies. In contrast, authentic enterprises live up to their values, truly appreciating their stakeholders and communicating that appreciation. In authentic enterprises there is an alignment between the stated vision and values with what is actually done day-to-day, as well as in how various stakeholders perceive the enterprise. Further, narrow conceptions of purpose, such as maximising shareholder wealth, tend not to create a sense of wholeness for others stakeholders. Rather than being inclusive, they are exclusive of the needs and interests of those other stakeholders. We believe that successful SEE Change enterprises negotiate the complexities of integrity and create value for all their stakeholders.

Human scale and scope

Writing in his *Wall Street Journal* blog, Janmejaya Sinha, Managing Director of the Boston Consulting Group India, points out that companies currently on the US Fortune 500 list are hardly permanent members of that list (Sinha 2009). As Sinha notes, even being the biggest is no guarantee of survival, never mind success. He further observes:

The market is supposed to sort this kind of thing out. But the real world is turning out to be a bit more complicated. Important intellectual questions are arising that need answers. When do the economies of scale clash with the economies of scope? At what size do traditional organisation structures start to creak? When does business complexity get too large to cope with? What is the extent of product complexity, geographic spread and employee workforce that is manageable? And most importantly, who bears the cost of failure?

In a fully realised sustainable enterprise economy, the days of the giant corporation would probably be numbered. Huge enterprises, no matter what sector they are in, tend to be dehumanised places in which to work. But as Sinha points out, the huge size of enterprises may also create a form of 'moral hazard', which is the lack of incentives to guard against risk because you are protected from it (e.g. by insurance). It is notable that many of the problems associated with the economic collapse of 2008–2009 were generated because few risks were perceived, creating moral hazards. Moral hazards are problematic because they create disconnects between decisions and actions (e.g. between management making the decisions and the stakeholders who will have to bear the costs of those decisions).

Of course, we witnessed these implications of non-human-sized enterprises numerous times during the economic meltdown of 2008; however, they were apparent to some observers long before that. They were manifested in the willingness of executives to lay-off staff time and again so that companies could be downsized or 'right'-sized during the 1980s and 1990s. They are consistently manifested in companies' willingness to spew pollutants into the environment, with little apparent regard for the consequences, or to engage suppliers whose employment practices are nothing short of abusive, or simply to 'outsource' jobs.

Alfred Chandler (1962) long ago documented the ability of corporations to grow larger as communication and transportation advances enabled executives to 'manage' enterprises of ever-larger scope. The advent of global and virtually instantaneous electronics communications, combined with air and other speedy forms of transport, have enabled enterprises to become global in scope. Indeed, one of the frequent comments during the economic crisis of 2008 was that certain enterprises had become 'too big to fail'. Of course the contrasting perspective was that those enterprises *should* be allowed to fail, simply because they were, in fact, too big to manage effectively. SEE Change enterprises need to find some way of managing their growth differently—to be successful without growing too big and without growth as the only goal.

Box 5 **Seventh Generation**[10]

Seventh Generation blends its profit-making goals with a mission to 'protect [the] world with . . . natural safe and effective household products'. Based in Burlington, Vermont, US, the company has declared itself to be socially responsible with core principles that focus 'on offering people avenues to express their idealism, passion and commitment to causes larger than themselves at every point along its supply chain—from suppliers and partners to shareholders, customers and its own staff'. The name of the company comes from the Iroquois Nation, which recognises that: 'In our every deliberation, we must consider the impact of our decisions on the next seven generations.' To accomplish its mission, Seventh Generation has developed non-toxic household products ranging from 100% recycled paper towels, bathroom and facial tissues to recycled plastic rubbish bags and chlorine-free nappies. By 2008, the company had 46% of the market share in its product categories, with operating income 600% up over 2001.

In an effort to live up to its ambitions, Seventh Generation issues an annual 'corporate consciousness' report that details both the pluses and minuses of its business operations, including a complete audit of its product ingredients, supply chain management practices and carbon footprint. In setting out its mission, it also recognises its participation in the broader system where there is significant need for change. Trying to do its part, Seventh Generation lists five 'global imperatives:' provide innovative solutions; inspire conscious consumption; create a just and equitable world; restore our environment; and work together.

SEE Change enterprise and economy

The characteristics of SEE Change enterprise and economy are quite different from what we have come to accept as normal in enterprise today. Focused on a just, equitable and more sustainable world, these enterprises are not content with growth for its own sake or at all costs. Their

10 www.seventhgeneration.com.

founders and members do not buy into a faster-is-always-better mentality, nor is profit the only motivation that such enterprises seek, although many do in fact seek to be profitable (see Box 5). Instead, their motives are more complex, their goals are more ambitious and ambiguous, and they often participate in multiple domains simultaneously. The next chapter will explore the leadership qualities that will be needed in the future to ensure the success of these emerging SEE Change enterprises.

9
Leading SEE Change

We need a new strategy for this economy. We should clear away any arrogance, false assumptions that things will be 'ok' if we stick to the status quo.

**Jeff Immelt, CEO and Chair, General Electric,
9 December 2009**[1]

The world is getting better, but it's not getting better fast enough, and it's not getting better for everyone. The great advances in the world have often aggravated the inequities in the world . . . The genius of capitalism lies in its ability to make self-interest serve the wider interest. The potential of a big financial return for innovation unleashes a broad set of talented people in pursuit of many different discoveries. This system, driven by self-interest, is responsible for the incredible innovations that have improved so many lives. But to harness this power so it benefits everyone, we need to refine the system . . . The challenge here is to design a system where market incentives, including profits and recognition, drive those principles to do more for the poor. I like to call this idea creative capitalism, an approach where governments, businesses and non-profits work together to stretch the reach of market forces so that more people can make

---

1 Jeff Immelt, 'Renewing American Leadership', files.gereports.com/wp-content/uploads/2009/12/90304-2-JRI-Speech-Reprint1-557.qxd_8.5x11.pdf, accessed 24 February 2010.

a profit, or gain recognition, doing work that eases the world's inequities.

Bill Gates, World Economic Forum, 24 January 2008[2]

We want to accelerate our efforts in sustainability. We want to broaden our efforts. It's not something of the past. This is all about the future.

Mike Duke, CEO, Wal-Mart, 29 January 2009[3]

What we see today is that people want a company they can trust and a transparent operation in addition to high-quality products and services. At the very bottom of the list are excellent numbers and a strong leader. So the values imply a change in what companies aim for.

Richard W. Edelman, President and CEO, Edelman, World Economic Forum, 28 January 2010[4]

The problem is making policy now for a problem that will not manifest itself for 30 to 40 years.

Tom Albanese, President and CEO, Rio Tinto, January 2010[5]

The need for new leadership in SEE Change

When leaders of major corporations that are deeply entrenched and successful in the current system acknowledge the need for significant change to deal with issues of sustainability, climate change, trust and equity, we know something important is beginning to happen. Collectively, the voices quoted at this chapter's opening are calling for systemic change.

2   Bill Gates, 'A New Approach to Capitalism for the 21st Century', www.microsoft.com/presspass/exec/billg/speeches/2008/01-24wefdavos.mspx, accessed 24 February 2010.
3   Mike Duke, 'Wal-Mart's New CEO to Ramp Up Sustainability Strategy', www.sustainablelifemedia.com/content/story/strategy/new_walmart_ceo_to_stay_course_on_sustainability, accessed 24 February 2010.
4   Richard W. Edelman, 'Rebuilding Trust in Business Leadership', www.weforum.org/pdf/AM_2010/transcripts/rebuilding-trust.pdf, accessed 25 February 2010.
5   Tom Albanese, 'The Future of Capitalism: Building a Sustainable Energy Future', www.mckinseyquarterly.com/The_future_of_capitalism_Building_a_sustainable_energy_future_2478, accessed 17 March 2011.

The old ways of enterprise, the old goals and the old leadership styles will need to be modified to cope with the significant changes that need to take place over the next few decades if humanity is to thrive and if capitalism is to be reformed.

In our rapidly changing, troubled times, the need for new leadership has never been more critical. The fourth report of the IPCC (2007), for example, called for rapid adaptation towards a much more sustainable way of enterprise. But who really knows how to achieve that level of sustainability or change the system in that direction? Coupled with this, is the diffusion of power away from the US as the world's sole super power towards an amalgam of the US, Europe, Japan, China, Russia, India and Brazil. This shift presents the challenge of who is to lead the fight for Earth's survival? How is that leadership to emerge? And, importantly, what type of leadership is needed?

One of our premises is that we already know much of what needs to be known to make the necessary changes. What is really needed (aside from a sharing of that knowledge) is the political will and public support for the shifts and changes that are necessary. We also need to find the appropriate path that, although likely to be resisted by those with vested interests in the current system, can ultimately move things forward.

Perhaps the global economic and financial crisis of late 2008 presents a blessing in disguise because, unlike the climate change crisis, the financial meltdown presented a crisis deep, visible and immediate enough that the imperative to act was obvious to any astute observer. What has become equally obvious, however, is the difficulty of actually engaging change from the top down when the elites (some might say the plutocracy or corporatocracy) who run the world continue to benefit from the current system. This is especially so since the change process itself will be very difficult. There are organisational, political, system, social and cultural changes that need to be made—and educational efforts will be needed to support these changes. That is why we believe that much of SEE Change will happen in both a top-down (from established institutions and organisations) and bottom-up (from the new types of social enterprises discussed earlier in this book) way, much along the creative destruction lines discussed by Schumpeter (1962).

We believe that future leaders will need several qualities if they are to be effective. First, and critically, they need to be systems thinkers who can understand interdependency and connections in the system as a whole and make links between what is done today and what happens tomorrow. Equally important, they will need to be collaborative rather than authoritarian in their approaches, and have enough self-efficacy, confidence and, ultimately, courage to be willing to take the necessary risks to make change happen.

People and their dreams

In our post-modern world of spin, anything goes, market-driven values and frenetic management styles, people want enterprises founded on integrity and clear values (McIntosh 2008; Waddock 2009). With integrity comes authenticity—a capacity to reflect on the consequences of action and make wise choices (Ackoff 1999). This combination of authenticity and integrity at the workplace resonates with many who aspire to meaningful work in meaningful enterprises. Too many types of work and workplaces are deeply dehumanising. We believe that SEE Change enterprises have the potential to change that situation, but to do so will require a mindset, approach and sense of purpose very different to that of many of today's large organisations.

There is a need to find more creative and systemic ways to deal with the many crises facing humanity and the environment. We need hope and optimism to move the world forwards. We need to ask: 'What kind of world do we want to live in? What world do we want to leave for our grandchildren?' As we have already seen, some of the new forms of SEE enterprise have begun to deal with these issues.

First, we need to recognise that building new dreams for the world is serious business that requires different leadership than we are used to. It will demand new ways of learning, sharing and problem-solving to find solutions to the humanitarian and ecological situations that face us all. Baker, Jensen and Kolb (2005) have developed work on conversational learning consistent with our work on sustainable enterprise. These approaches mean doing work that is based on co-sensing, co-inspiring, co-enacting and co-creating knowledge. Second, the world requires knowledge creation that sees both hard and soft edges (and can work with both equally well), that can sense the tangible and the intangible, that is both left- and right-brained, and that is founded on what is known but also reaches into the energy of the complexity and apparent chaos for new ideas. We live in an age of reconfiguration, of decay and resurgence, a state where new value clusters are being created through the realignment of social networks and public–private–civil partnerships. Enterprise, innovation, creativity and action are creating a new economy that is at once local *and* global, founded on a greater understanding of organisations as living social systems nested within living organic eco-systems. With this understanding not only is the way we learn changing, but what we think is useful is also being challenged.

This challenge is perhaps best described by David Cooperrider, the originator of 'appreciative inquiry' who inspired the following approach (Barrett and Fry 2005: 33-35):

> We have become so locked within a problem-centred, critique-driven worldview that we have severely limited out potential for innovation and transformation . . . New understanding emerges when we begin our capacity-building through welcoming the unknown as an opportunity for discovery and innovation. It means suspending our confidence in old certainties.

Third, we face some imperatives. The imperatives of the sustainable enterprise agenda call for us to find ways to free ourselves from want and fear. These imperatives mean addressing issues such as poverty, violence, inequity, discrimination and human rights within our enterprise models. They mean finding positive ways to build just and peaceful societies. They mean acknowledging that life is based on the principle of co-creation, hence our emphasis on knowledge creation through conversational learning which draws on experiential learning, action research and appreciative inquiry.

There are some people who insist on maintaining the myth that there is an incompatibility between 'green growth' and comfort, or between economic wealth creation and sustainability. We believe otherwise. Significant work is now going on to motivate change towards what is loosely termed 'the green economy'. In some cases, recovery from the 2008 economic collapse and recognition of climate change have been linked to moves towards a low carbon sustainable enterprise economy. Indeed some of the best research is being carried out by those global institutions that are most affected by the current revolution. Among these institutions is one of the world's largest banks, HSBC, a bank that has not been carrying toxic debts to any substantial degree. Its team, led by Nick Robins, published a study of 20 national economic recovery plans in February 2009. The leaders turned out to be the US and China, with key beneficiaries of recovery efforts being rail transportation, water infrastructure and improved building efficiency.

The research identified 18 investment themes that can be identified with 'stabilising and then cutting global emissions of greenhouse gases' representing 15% of the US$2.8 trillion in fiscal measures to restart national economies. The 18 themes include: low-carbon energy, including renewables and nuclear power; energy efficiency and management, including goods and services that enhance building, industrial and transport efficiency, and energy storage; water, waste and pollution control, including water conservation, treatment and supply; and carbon finance, especially carbon markets (Robins *et al.* 2009).

In March 2009, Rajendra Pachauri, Chair of the IPCC and winner of the Nobel Peace Prize 2008, commented on the link between sustainable enterprise economics and wellbeing:[6]

> The beauty of (the) desirable changes lies in the fact that they would produce a huge range of so called co-benefits which, if anything, will enhance the welfare of human society such as through higher energy security, lower levels of pollution at the local level, stable agricultural yields and additional employment. I wonder why we are dragging our feet in the face of such overwhelming logic?

The answer to Pachauri's own question lies in the lack of real leadership among politicians and business leaders. As he says:

> The answer lies in forward looking policies on the part of governments, which of course will cause some discomfort in certain sectors and to certain actors. A complete reorientation of thinking among the leadership of the corporate sector and a significant change in lifestyles of people across the globe, most importantly in the rich countries, is now overdue. If a perceptible shift in all these three respects can be initiated adequately ... future generations would have reason to thank those that bring about such a movement.

At the UN Global Compact Leaders Summit in Geneva on 9 July 2007, Pachauri outlined a six-point plan of action:

- Invest heavily in energy conservation, eco-efficiency and sustainable design;
- Introduce comprehensive carbon pricing;
- Dramatically improve water efficiency;

---

6 blog.pachauri.org/blog/13/Why-Copenhagen-is-important-for-the-future-of-human-civilisation-htm.

- Induce life style and behavioural changes;

- Adapt to climate change now;

- Leave no one behind.

Since November 2007, when the IPCC released its fourth assessment, many forward-looking government's have taken up the challenge including China and Australia. For all of us to live like an American or an Australian, we would need four planets. We would need two planets for all of us to live like a European or a New Zealander. We also need to remember that China, like most of Europe, has already managed to bring birth and population growth rates down, while also raising life expectancy dramatically.

The sustainable enterprise economy is not, we believe, an economy in which people will be worse off than their parents. It is not an economy where comfort is sacrificed. It is not an economy where mobility is denied. Nor does it need larger populations and constant 'growth'. Indeed, the world's population probably needs to shrink considerably over the next two generations for the Earth to be able to support it adequately.

The Optimum Population Trust asks people to pledge to have no more than two children, but does not support enforced family planning. Its research shows that the world's population needs to halve to about 3 billion. It argues that in the face of the climate change challenge, migration is the equivalent of 'moving the deckchairs on the Titanic'. Yet there are still many countries seeking to *increase* their populations, most notably the UK from 60 million to 77 million, and Australia from 20 million to more than 30 million by 2025.[7] Given the impact of expanding populations on the planet and biodiversity, the founder of WWF, Sir Peter Scott, has been quoted as saying: 'I have often thought that, at the end of the day, we [WWF] would have saved more wildlife if we had spent all WWF's money on buying condoms.'[8]

We believe that humans are engaged in humankind's fourth 'great transformation'. First was the agricultural revolution; second came industrialisation; third was the information age. Now we face the age of sustainability—learning to live within the Earth's limits. We humans have in many respects been fantastically successful—we have conquered and controlled our environment, and we breed like rabbits! Now is the time to include population control in the list of issues that must be faced if we are

7 www.optimumpopulation.org, accessed 20 May 2009.
8 www.population.org.au, accessed 10 June 2010.

to develop the sustainable enterprise economy. The following five issues are, we believe, universal and relevant to all governments, companies and individuals:

- Democratic, transparent and accountable governance mechanisms are needed for all organisations and institutions in society, with a corresponding respect for human rights and an absence of corruption;

- We must adapt to climate change, and we must do so now;

- We must be more efficient with our use of energy and more intelligent in our production of energy;

- We must be much more water efficient;

- We need to lower the total world population by discouraging families from having more than two children.

The sustainable enterprise leader

SEE Change has significant implications for the type of leader needed in the future. If the 20th century was the era of 'tough' leadership, perhaps the new millennium can bring a different definition of what it means to lead, one that is inherently more collaborative, able to cope with differences and willing to adapt to an uncertain future. Below we briefly highlight some of the characteristics that we believe SEE Change will demand of its leaders and entrepreneurs (Waddock and McIntosh 2009).

Boundary spanning

Many people succeed with skills that are built upon a basis of functional expertise, at least to a certain level in their enterprises. Beyond that, as discussed earlier, succeeding in the ambiguous future of SEE Change will demand the capacity to cross boundaries. In the world of SEE Change, there will be many enterprises that cross traditional sector boundaries, and within them, there will be an increasing need to cross functional boundaries as well, particularly if the systemic implications of actions and decisions are to be understood.

While narrow specialisation in a functional or technical area can be useful as an early career strategy, it will become more and more difficult to succeed at the enterprise level without a greater systems orientation. Thus, the ability to manage across sectors, functions and types of enterprises, to understand the perspectives of many different stakeholders who come to the table with a wide spectrum of different ideologies, values, decision-making styles and capabilities, will be integral to success. Managing multiple bottom lines inherently means crossing sector boundaries. Because SEE Change enterprises draw from the strengths of different sectors (which means that their weaknesses will also be evident), it will be important for leaders to understand those strengths and weaknesses so they can be used effectively. Because globalisation is unlikely to disappear, it will also be important for leaders to understand not just other sectors, but also different cultures, ethnic groups, and societal norms and values.

Systems thinking

Systems thinking is a capacity that not everyone possesses and that seems to be associated with higher levels of cognitive development. Yet it is clear to us that the capacity for systems thinking and understanding is an imperative for the future and for SEE Change to become fully realised. A stakeholder orientation, which SEE Change enterprises inherently have, demands the capacity to take different perspectives, so that stakeholder points of view can be understood and, where appropriate, incorporated into the enterprise. Engaging with stakeholders necessitates systems thinking since different stakeholders have different perspectives, ideologies, ideas, cultures, norms, values and understandings. For engagement with stakeholders to truly work, leaders need to have the capacity to truly understand 'where they are coming from' so that when differences arise, as they inevitably will, they can be handled effectively.

We believe that such capabilities can be developed by continually exposing people not just to the linear production models and narrowly defined problems that underlie most Western educational models, but to rather more undefined open-ended problems. People need to be exposed to whole system applications and understandings that follow, for example, the logical progression of a decision or a product, from its raw materials source to its end-of-life disposal—either into a waste site or as 'food' for another system. The idea that what is waste for one system becomes food for another is a fundamental concept to which future leaders need consistent and ongoing exposure, and is a core element of systems thinking.

Other methods for developing whole systems perspectives include exposure to natural systems, in-depth exploration of cultures beyond one's own, questioning of the assumptions beneath decisions and existing systems, and efforts to follow through the consequences of those systems. There are numerous other ways to develop more systems thinking capacity in future leaders, such as future search exercises, creating mind maps, using open space designs and world café formats discussed earlier in the book.

Capacity for collaboration *and* competition

Because SEE Change enterprises have multiple bottom lines and cross sector boundaries, they are also likely to be engaged with other enterprises in collaborative efforts. Particularly because the social and ecological problems that they address are broadly conceived, the ability to collaborate as well as compete becomes critical.

Unlike competition, collaboration means engaging with more stakeholders—and understanding their perspectives so that when appropriate they can be built into the enterprise's activities. Collaborative approaches demand great listening skills, as well as high degrees of emotional intelligence, particularly when collaborators differ, so that the message behind what is being stated or demanded can be understood.

Integrity

Most people in business or any other enterprise today would argue that integrity is important, and many businesses claim to seek integrity in their business operations and leader. The numerous scandals of the early 2000s and the systemic failures that became evident in the economic collapse of 2008, suggest that integrity is actually sorely lacking in far too many institutions. Part of the problem is that narrow goals associated with short-term profit maximisation push people to make decisions with long-term or systemically negative consequences. As a result, public trust in business has fallen to an all-time low. These scandals caused great concern, especially in the US, about extraordinarily high levels of chief executive remuneration that seemed totally unwarranted and unjust, especially when compared to what the average worker earns.

Individual integrity is as critical to developing and maintaining trust within systems as system integrity as a whole is to maintaining trust in the system itself. Integrity in all of its definitions—honesty, wholeness, maintaining a strong ethical code—is one of the fundamentals of SEE Change leadership, particularly since there are inherent complexities in these enterprises, because of their boundary spanning and multiple goals. Only leaders with integrity will be able to succeed in such enterprises over the long term.

Comfort with ambiguity

The nature of SEE Change enterprises—collaborative, blended value bottom-lines encompassing social/ecological goals and benefits, sometimes with a profit orientation and boundary spanning—also means that future leaders need well-developed comfort with ambiguity. SEE Change enterprise is more organic and chaotic in its growth and development; hence there is likely to be a great deal of ambiguity to manage. Individuals nurtured in typical MBA programmes will likely be less successful than those who have coped with the complexities and ambiguities of problem finding by tackling messy real-world problems in their educational paths, or who have tried to create new solutions to messy problems (Cheit 1984). SEE Change enterprise problems are often 'messy' (Ackoff 1975), requiring non-linear, collaborative and design-driven solutions.

Courage to be a change agent

One key attribute that future leaders will need is the courage and capacity to be a change agent, both within their own enterprises as well as in the broader societies where they operate. Since 'business' is likely to be unusual in SEE Change, the change process is an important element of establishing any SEE Change enterprise. Not only will leaders need the creativity to see what needs to be done (which requires a systems orientation and understanding), but they will also need to find the inner resources to do things in a different way by breaking with the past. Sometimes SEE Change entrepreneurs will have to fight established entities and systems, sometimes they will have to step outside the box to see what might be done. This requires courage, imagination and a sense of self-efficacy, as well as the ability to enrol others in their sense of purpose and mission. Research indicates that courageous leaders are in rather short supply (Blowfield and Googins 2006). In addition, they will need to be agents of change, with the political and organisational development skills to lead internal and external change, and be able to recognise and enrol allies in that change process. Change in large institutions is inherently difficult, perhaps even as difficult as growing small institutions with SEE Change criteria built in. Both aspects of leading in SEE Change demand the capacity to effect change with considerably more skill than has been needed in the past.

Future orientation

Typically problem-solvers look to find answers from the present and the past, but SEE Change leaders will also need a future orientation to think through the consequences of their decisions not just for the short term, but for future generations. Greater enhancement of a systems orientation will enhance this capacity, but more is needed. A sense of history is nevertheless necessary to develop a futures orientation because to know the past is to be able to recognise trends and opportunities that others might miss, and avoid repeating mistakes.

Hopeful myths and stories that create meaning on a human scale

Along with purposes that are inspirational, many SEE Change enterprises implicitly or explicitly attempt to create a sense of hope that they can make the world a better place. SEE Change enterprises are all about creating new vision and hope—developing a narrative or myth about the possibility that humankind can create a sustainable future. This contrasts with the current economics- and finance-centred mythology that the sole purpose of enterprise is to make a profit. The myth that is now emerging accepts the multiplicity of bottom-lines inherent in combining economic imperatives with social justice or ecological goals. Goals can involve economic stability, meeting unmet social needs, helping people at the bottom-of-the-pyramid live better lives, providing jobs and job stability, and balancing the interests of humans with those of nature.

Whatever form they take, organisations in a sustainable enterprise economy need to be human-scaled in ways that fill their participants with focus, purpose and meaning, rather than being the soul-deadening enterprises that so many are today. This approach may mean that local needs trump global wherever feasible, with the recognition that global enterprise is most likely here to stay.

In summary, humanity needs human-scale organisations that have at their heart planetary imperatives. We need enterprises with sustainable values that serve society rather than exploit it. We need enterprises that put integrity and trust at the heart of decision-making processes. This shift means a greater emphasis on accountability, responsibility and assurance, as well as on organisational transparency. Further, there needs to be a well-considered rewriting of the rules of incorporation for business enterprises that refocuses them on their public interest purposes. But first there must be an emphasis on learning and education in business and across society as a whole.

Former UN Secretary-General Kofi Annan said in January 1999, on the launch of the Global Compact: 'Let us choose to unite the power of markets with the authority of universal ideals. Let us choose to reconcile the creative forces of private entrepreneurship with the needs of the disadvantaged and the requirements of future generations.' We can further add: let us choose to unite the power of markets and the creativity of the human spirit with the authority of universal ideals. Let us choose to reconcile the creative forces of private and public and social entrepreneurship with the needs of the disadvantaged and the requirements of future generations.

Facing the challenge

The challenge for society and for communities all over the world is enormous, but we have no choice, it must be met. It has been argued in the past that the information age and our understanding of complex systems mean we can ride the waves of change. In a book entitled *The Collapse of Complex Societies* Joseph Sainter argued (1990):

> Complex societies are characterised by central decision-making, high information flow, great coordination of parts, formal channels of command and pooling of resources. Dealing with adverse environmental conditions may be what complex societies do best.

Jared Diamond's 2005 monumental study into communities that have disappeared argued something completely different. In *Collapse: How Societies Choose to Fail or Survive* Diamond posited four main reasons why various peoples had stopped flourishing in various communities around the world over the last few thousand years:

> 'Creeping normalcy' . . . change that is slow enough for peo-
> ple to think that how it is now is how it always was; 'Landscape
> amnesia' . . . people forget how the land used to look, or where
> the trees used to be, and when the birds used to sing; 'Rational
> behaviour' . . . people stop being emotional or spiritual or sacred
> because we are bound to find a techno-fix or a sensible way out;
> 'It's someone else's problem' . . . the sense that there is little that
> I can do about the situation anyway.

We need to ask ourselves how many of these conditions exist for us today.
Here is an example that may help. In 1991 a man's body emerged from a
melting glacier on the Austro-Italian border in the Alps. Otzi, as he became
known, turned out to be more than 5,000 years old and had been quick
frozen, which meant that he had been perfectly preserved. His clothes
and body were intact and his stomach contained the remains of his last
meal. In *The Man in the Ice,* Konrad Spindler (1995) brought Otzi's Neo-
lithic world to life. In doing so, he highlighted our modern dilemma—that
we are distanced from the environment that sustains us:

> In the agricultural society of the Neolithic an individual would
> possess the total knowledge of his period, as well as all the skills
> necessary to perform his daily tasks. He would know how to
> hunt, fish and gather food, how to till his field, look after his live-
> stock and build huts. He would make his own pots, prepare his
> food and manufacture the tools and implements needed for all
> these activities.

While we make no suggestion that we should return to this way of life,
what is clear is that we have lost our connection to the origins of our sustenance—to nature. That reality is highlighted in *Last Child in the Woods*
by Richard Louv (2005). Louv argues that humans—and especially children—in the developed world are increasingly disconnected from nature
and are suffering from what he terms 'nature deficit disorder'. When—not
if—the oil runs out, how many people will survive? Probably only those
who live close to the earth and who have the skills and knowledge to grow
and hunt their own food.

The first priority in developing a sustainable enterprise economy is
to recognise what Keynes said just before World War II, that economic
growth is not an end in itself but a means to 'the enjoyments and realities of life' (Keynes 1932). Barbara Ward reminds us that we have 'only one
Earth' (Ward and Dubos 1972). We need to: strive for better local and global governance of people, planet and wellbeing; adapt to climate change;

conserve energy and water; and control the global human population. These are the priorities for humanity today.

10

Towards a sustainable enterprise economy

Ten years after the launch of the Global Compact, its Executive Head Georg Kell argued that real changes in the relationship between businesses and society had been made, noting that the notion of CR had become global in scope, and that global integration had 'triggered convergence around values and principles'.[1] As evidence for this, he pointed to the numerous companies with human rights policies—unheard of ten years earlier. He also noted that many elements of progressive CR can be seen not just in developed but, importantly, in emerging markets. Further, non-financial reporting is growing and CR is informing governance voices in the global arena, with elements of ESG being incorporated as a normal part of doing business.

Despite his optimism about the progress of CR, particularly as evidenced through the UN Global Compact, Kell pointed out that 'much work remains to be done to lay the foundation for an age of global prosperity and peaceful cooperation'. In looking ahead, Kell made seven critical points about the future that lays the foundation for the present chapter. First, despite progress in embedding CR in some companies, particularly

---

1 Georg Kell, 'Ten Years After', Chatham House, 13 March 2008; available at www. ethicalmarkets.com/2008/03/13/"ten-years-after-georg-kells-speech-at-chatham-house, accessed 12 March 2011.

the Compact's signatories, there remain many businesses not committed to responsible corporate practice. Committed companies therefore need to spread the CR message throughout their subsidiaries and supply chains. He also argued that it is important to 'nurture the emerging link between responsible investment and CR', as a means of further establishing the business case.

Kell also pointed out the importance of continuing convergence around globally accepted frameworks (rather than continued proliferation of such frameworks). He particularly noted the importance of the ISO 26000 CR standards 'as a practical tool for implementing globally established instruments'. Further, Kell stated: 'We must welcome efforts by new entrants to embrace CR, while also providing incentives that motivate front runners to keep pace and give direction.' Finally, Kell pointed out the importance of civil society's continuing vigilance and highlighted the complementary relationship that exists between regulatory and voluntary approaches, along with the need to continue to develop new approaches to the problems that have already emerged and continue to evolve in the world.

Kell's comments, along with the evidence we have presented earlier, suggest the importance of system change, not only for large well-established companies and that may or may not be adopting CR strategies, but also for the many emerging enterprises in the sustainable enterprise economy. In this new economy, the tenets of capitalism as we have known it are being called into question.

What has evolved in the past few decades is not a capitalism in which products and services are being provided to customers with needs and demands. Rather, it is a form of financial capitalism that distorts incentives, rewards the already well-off, and cares little for the externalities it creates or for the nature, quality, longevity or usefulness of its products and services. It is a capitalism that assumes that the weakened government it has essentially demanded through, for example, the Bretton Woods institutions, will pick up the pieces and simply create social justice and sustainability. That form of capitalism is no longer tenable in light of the financial meltdown of 2008 and the impending sustainability crises, although some attempts at reform are being made.

Speaking in Paris in August 2009 at the opening of the economic symposium *New World, New Capitalism*, French President Nicolas Sarkozy framed the problem:[2]

2 'French, German Leaders Call for "Moralisation" of Capitalism', 1 August 2009, www.dw-world.de/dw/article/0,,3930542,00.html, accessed 25 February 2010.

> Purely financial capitalism has perverted the logic of capitalism. Financial capitalism is a system of irresponsibility and . . . is amoral. It is a system where the logic of the market excuses everything . . . Either we re-found capitalism or we destroy it.

Along much the same lines, German Chancellor Angela Merkel called for a 'charter for a long-term reasonable economy' like that of the UN, and noted:[2]

> There is a risk that when everything is functioning normally again that the financial institutions will tell politicians not to meddle. We must remain determined.

A sustainable enterprise economy will produce benefits in the form of private wealth *and* public goods (Bendell *et al.* 2010). That is the central premise of SEE Change, as we discuss below.

The sustainable enterprise economy

The main tenets of the industrial era economy on which today's economic system is built are no longer viable in the resource-constrained, connected and complex world we now live in (Toffler 1984). Industrial era organisations, particularly modern corporations, are premised on maxims of growth and efficiency (Frederick 1995), a linear production model and a narrow focus on shareholder interests. These emphases have meant that a highly competitive, growth-at-all-costs orientation, is deeply embedded in the economic system and corporation structures.

In this economic system, governments set the rules and businesses then work around the rules to accomplish what management theorist William Frederick (1995) calls their 'economising' goals, which may mean outsourcing production, externalising pollution and other costs, or squeezing out competitors. A sustainable enterprise *economy*, we will argue below, has different objectives and agendas—and will need a different managerial mindset and set of leadership skills to carry it off. Below we will explore some of the emerging characteristics of this new economy.

Economic stability not growth

Too much of what is produced today is the result of a growth-at-all costs mentality that is ecologically unsupportable in a resource-constrained world projected to have more than nine billion people by 2050. Too many of these products are built for short-term or planned obsolescence, fostering ever greater consumption, and continually growing the bottom-line. Too many enterprises have become 'too big to fail' in ways that are creating obvious social and economic problems. We believe that the problems of managing truly global enterprises need to be recognised and dealt with by instilling a new mindset around stability, the fundamental basis of sustainability, rather than growth.

To sustain something is not necessarily to grow it, but rather to preserve its integrity over time, providing nourishment rather than deprivation. Underlying the concept of sustainability is a sense of equity among the peoples of the world and, arguably, other species as well. Achieving sustainability will not be easy for those with affluent lifestyles who will have to moderate their consumption so that others can access some of the planet's resources.

Unspoken in much of the conversation about sustainability is the need to control population growth. Some ecologists estimate that the world can sustainably support somewhere between two and three billion people, but the planetary population is already nearing seven billion. Issues of population growth, complex as they are, underlie the vision of SEE Change enterprises for equity and sustainability.

Moving away from a growth-at-all costs enterprise orientation will be a difficult shift of mind, or what Peter Senge (1990) calls a 'metanoia'. But the ecological constraints now confronting us suggest that a metanoia is needed if humanity is to thrive in a future fraught with resource constraints. Larger enterprises, particularly businesses, need to learn from the many millions of small and medium-sized enterprises with stable incomes that have been in existence for years, providing local jobs, sourcing more or less locally, and serving relatively local or regional markets quite happily.

Yet, more is needed. SEE Change is actually about finding ways for humanity to thrive not just sustain, and for the Earth's other species to thrive too. A hopeful development is the growing recognition that wealth is no longer about having a lot of money; rather, it is about wellbeing and happiness.

Success as wellbeing

The shift away from a constant growth orientation suggests the need to redefine what success actually means. If growth—in market share, profits or size—is not to be the measure of success, then what is? We argue that we need to find better measures of wellbeing—for individuals, communities, enterprises and for the planet—and that wellbeing, not growth, should become the mantra of enterprise. Analysts should be asking: 'How much wellbeing has your enterprise created?' Many of today's large enterprises and financial institutions in particular would not fare very well in answering that question.

One purpose of the sustainable enterprise economy is job and economic stability rather than growth at all costs. The UN estimates that some 1.4 billion young people are seeking work or will be in the next few years. 'Decent work', as the International Labour Organisation calls it, is important for people to feel they are leading productive and meaningful lives. Sustainable enterprise, with its human-scaled enterprises, may be part of the answer to this problem—creating greater levels of wellbeing.

The New Economics Foundation created the Happy Planet Index (HPI) in 2006[3] to provide an alternative to traditional economic measures of wellbeing. The HPI does not actually measure happiness as such; rather, it focuses on the ecological efficiency of delivering wellbeing in different countries. It looks at how efficiently countries convert their natural resources to better lives for their citizens. In 2009 the HPI judged Costa Rica as the most ecologically efficient country: 'Costa Ricans live slightly longer than Americans and report much higher levels of life satisfaction, and yet have a[n ecological] footprint which is less than a quarter the size.'

The notion of wellbeing in practice may mean that the goal of growth itself is recognised as unrealistic. This new understanding is implicit in the HPI as well as similar indicators that go beyond GDP, such as the Calvert-Henderson Index or the Genuine Progress Indicator. In an era when too many businesses are deemed to be 'too big to fail', and where limits to continued growth are more readily recognised, perhaps the mantra of growth itself must end. A better framework for thinking about going forward might be the idea of economic stability—creating a balance between fair returns to investors and to the other stakeholders that comprise the enterprise.

3 www.happyplanetindex.org.

Local trumps global

In recent years, there has been a considerable movement toward locali-sation, at least of food and related products. This idea neatly aligns with other emerging ideas and movements, such as the 'slow food movement'. More radical approaches to reorganising the world, such as articulated by Cavanagh *et al.* (2002) or David Korten in his book *Agenda for a New Economy* (2010), suggest that globalisation is not, as many people think, inevitable. Rather, it has been designed by the Bretton Woods organisa-tions (IMF, WTO and the World Bank) along with industrialised nations that make up the powerful elements of their membership.

Such a perspective suggests that, while globalisation is unlikely to go away, a move towards more local and regional production of goods and services would be healthier for the planet and its people. An example of 'local trumping global' is BALLE (Business Alliance for Local Living Economies)[4] which promotes the idea of local businesses using local resources as far as possible. It has taken off in the US and now has dozens of local networks. BALLE believes that healthy local businesses can trans-form communities, making them the kinds of places that people want to live, and creating prosperous and thriving economic and social envi-ronments. BALLE considers that: 'The primary purpose of a true market economy is not to make money for the rich and powerful.'

When Adam Smith (1776) conceptualised the idea of the market econ-omy in his classic *The Wealth of Nations,* he had in mind economies that allocate human and material resources justly and sustainably to meet the self-defined needs of people and community. Similarly, BALLE believes that locally rooted businesses better serve their communities than unrooted businesses, that equity and democracy best serve the interests of community members and that, combined, these factors will give peo-ple more control over their lives through more job security, stable eco-nomic conditions and a more sustainable environment.

Society/nature's interests aligned with human interests

Overall, the sustainable enterprise economy marries goals such as the Millennium Development Goals (MDGs) into the goals of the enterprise itself. The MDGs are intended to improve the conditions of the nearly three billion people in the world estimated to be living in poverty. For some SEE

4 www.livingeconomies.org, accessed 23 July 2009.

Change enterprises, the MDG goals are also connected to principles like the UN Global Compact's or some other set of global standards, such as the OECD Guidelines on Multinational Enterprise or the Caux Roundtable's Principles, that provide similar guidance around core values.

Concerns about social justice and poverty suggest that these issues will need to be incorporated more explicitly into the goals and objectives of many different types of enterprise, including traditional businesses. Although the notion of social and ecological goals mixed with economic ones may seem difficult to achieve, the numerous social enterprises discussed earlier, as well as the legacy purpose of the corporation as serving the public interest, suggest that such multiple bottom lines are indeed feasible and socially productive. As we have seen, many businesses have already begun implementing social and environmental goals into their business goals, sometimes through CR programmes, sometimes through social entrepreneurial initiatives and sometimes because it is simply an integral part of the make-up of the business.

Future preserving

The sustainable enterprise economy needs to be oriented towards the future, and especially the future health of humanity and the Earth. To achieve that goal, people will need to come together in very different ways than they have in the past. The fundamental question for the future is: 'How can people learn?' What new ways of learning and planning for the future can be developed? Where do we start? With children and young adults or with elders? Given the urgency of the situation, it is likely that we will face the dual task of teaching both the young and the old simultaneously. In addition, we need to re-educate future leaders and managers of enterprises.

Real education leads to adaptation and survival, to the recognition of newly evolving forms, to an understanding of the system dynamics in which we are embedded, and to a capacity to take multiple perspectives simultaneously. These capacities are the hallmarks of individuals who have reached post-conventional levels of development. Indeed, some developmental psychologists suggest that while most people operate cognitively at conventional levels of development, there needs to be a shift towards more developed post-conventional levels of capacity (Kegan 1982; Torbert *et al.* 2004).

Education is more crucial than ever. We need to embrace a love of learning and accept change even in the face of uncertainty. Many more people need to develop the ability to move out of their comfort zones so that we can adapt to climate change, and so that we can together implement agreed upon sustainable development goals and deliver the MDGs.

Individuals at the conventional level of cognitive (and moral) development do not question the goals of either their group (e.g. local community, religion, ethnic or tribe) or their society (Kohlberg 1973, 1976; Kegan 1982; Torbert *et al.* 2004). Yet developmental theorist Robert Kegan (1982) points out that the complexities of modern life virtually demand that people move through the conventional to post-conventional levels of thinking. Only by doing so can they begin to take on multiple perspectives simultaneously and understand the fundamental principles that guide the system. Only with such deep understanding can real change begin.

At this level of cognition the capacity to understand the system—and potentially change it—begins to develop. All children begin their lives at the same pre-conventional levels of cognitive development and all must go through the nested sequence of stages to conventional (and post-conventional) thinking (Wilber 1995, 2002; Kegan 1982). The fact that so many people are beginning to question the system and working to change it from the inside is heartening. SEE Change enterprises of various kinds represent a hopeful sign that more people are reaching (or beginning to reach) post-conventional thinking.

The system changes needed call for a major relearning process that puts companies and other enterprises at the service of society not vice versa as has been the case recently. How can this relearning process be achieved? One example comes from the spread of CR and sustainability within multinational corporations during the late 1990s and early years of the new century. Many people believe that 'corporate responsibility' is an oxymoron. Yet on numerous occasions, we have seen high-profile corporations responding to criticism about their practices with CR initiatives. And these initiatives have been implemented on a voluntary basis, despite the fundamental structure and purpose of the corporation remaining unchanged. Arguably, such shifts will not be sufficiently long-lasting without underpinning by legislative and regulatory reform. However, they do suggest that even large companies are beginning to sense the need for change and are responding accordingly.

These initiatives, when they work, go well beyond the window dressing that companies are frequently accused of with respect to their corporate citizenship practices. Nike, for example, was castigated for poor supply chain practices and labour abuses in the 1990s, but has now taken the lead in monitoring and improving its own supply chains (though it is still not without supply chain problems). Similarly, giant chemical manufacturer Dow has what is probably one of the most progressive sustainability programmes of any companies, aiming not just to do less harm but actively to do good. And Coca-Cola, criticised for poor water resource use in India, has transformed its water policies and practices, making them central strategic issues for the future.

Other examples come from individuals who question the fundamentals of the current system and who work either from inside or outside the system to change it; Waddock (2008b) has called such individuals 'difference makers'. NGO leaders such as Peter Eigen and Frank Vogl who co-founded Transparency International, Odet Grajev, who founded The Ethos Institute in Brazil, and Italy's Giovanni Moro who founded the Active Citizen's Organisation, are such difference makers. They are far from alone. At the local and regional levels, as well as through the global action networks (GANs) discussed in Chapter 7, thousands, if not millions of people are involved in NGOs, CSOs, inter-governmental organisations and activist organisations. Paul Hawken (2008) calls this civil society movement 'blessed unrest' and we have labelled the broader movement that involves business SEE Change.

Competition and collaboration

One interesting thing about SEE Change is that it is premised, as are biological systems, as much on cooperation and collaboration (interdependencies) as on competition. Competition will not go away as SEE Change continues to evolve, just as it does not ever fully go away in natural systems. But as naturalists know, without cooperation (symbiosis in the biological framing), many organisations—indeed perhaps all living organisms—could not survive. In natural systems, as Hawken and other ecologists remind us, there is a web of life that connects organisms together in a web of interdependencies (Hawken 1993; Capra 1995; Hawken, Lovins and Lovins 1999; Lipton and Bhaerman 2009).

Human existence and the business system are similarly interdependent with other living beings on the planet for their wellbeing (Frederick 1995). This interdependence—and our recognition of it—is only heightened by the World Wide Web. That network of electronic connectivity now unites humanity in what we earlier described as the 'cloud' in which much of human knowledge is connected and where future capacity for sustainable change can potentially be found. SEE Change enterprise is emerging organically from the types of enterprises that currently exist, as well as creating wholly new forms with multiple bottom lines and an orientation toward ecological and social benefits.

Chances are (with any luck) that cooperation and collaboration will be as much a part of SEE Change as is competition. Today, many different organisations and sectors are working together in alliances, partnerships and informal collaborations on particular issues and initiatives. Concerns still exist about how competitive or vested interests can be overcome to meet sustainability challenges and create the new systems that the future demands. But the innovations are coming so rapidly that we believe there is yet hope for real systemic change.

Slow down, reflect, find balance

One of the characteristics of the modern economic system is its frenetic dynamism. The fast pace, constant change, increasing demand for 'new' things creates an ever-changing environment with chaos and discord at its heart. Yet the human soul craves green spaces, quiet time for reflection, and connection with other people and with nature (see, for example, Louv 2005). Wellbeing and the wisdom so desperately needed to better lead and manage our world cannot be attained when everything is on-the-go and constantly shifting. Sustainability—stability and sustenance—means finding time to slow down, reflect and bring sanity back into the system.

Bringing sanity back into the broader system probably means not wanting so much 'stuff', at least for those of us in the developed world. It may mean finding time for play as well as work, for interpersonal relationships as well as electronic connections. It may mean finding time for activities that grow us as people even if not in a career sense. In short, SEE Change may mean finding a new sense of balance in order to effect real change.

Towards a sustainable enterprise economy

Not all enterprises are sustainable or socially beneficial. Even so, most companies contribute to society through the provision of goods or services, and by providing employment. As we have seen, there are many other types of organisations being created today that deliver distinctive social and environmental as well as economic benefits. The concept of a sustainable enterprise is very wide-ranging.

In thinking about sustainable enterprise, we are essentially thinking about our relationship with the planet and with each other. There are serious challenges ahead. Currently, 30%–50% of humanity struggle with poverty, violence, oppression and a lack of access to basic resources. A 2003 UN report of human security by Sadako Ogata and Amartya Sen called for 'integrated policies that focus on people's survival, livelihood and dignity, during downturns as well as in prosperity' (Commission on Human Security 2003: iv). In other words we are all in this together. We hope that SEE Change provides an opportunity for all of us to rise to the challenge of creating a new, sustainable and life-giving world in which we can thrive together.

'We shall not cease from exploration / And the end of all our exploring / Will be to arrive where we started / And know the place for the first time.'[5]

---

5 T.S. Eliot, 'Little Gidding' (No. 4 of the Four Quartets).

Bibliography

Abadie, A. (2006) 'Poverty, Political Freedom and the Roots of Terrorism', *The American Economic Review* 96.2: 50-56.

Ackoff, R. (1975) *Redesigning the Future* (New York: Wiley).

—— (1999) 'On Learning and the Systems that Facilitate It', *Reflections* 1.1: 14-24.

Anand, S., and A. Sen (2000) 'Human Development and Economic Sustainability', *World Development* 28.12: 2029-49.

Annan, K. (1999) 'Business and the UN: A Global Compact of Shared Values and Principles', World Economic Forum, Davos, Switzerland, 31 January 1999, reprinted in *Vital Speeches of the Day* 65.9, 15 February 1999.

—— (2004) 'Foreword and the UN Global Compact', in M. McIntosh, S. Waddock and G. Kell (eds.), *Learning To Talk: Corporate Citizenship and the Development of the UN Global Compact* (Sheffield, UK: Greenleaf Publishing).

Appleyard, B. (2009) 'A guide to the 100 best blogs: part I', *Sunday Times*, 15 February 2009, technology.timesonline.co.uk/tol/news/tech_and_web/the_web/article5725644.ece.

Bakan, J. (2004) *The Corporation: The Pathological Pursuit of Profit and Power* (New York: Free Press).

Baker, A.C., P.J. Jensen and D.A. Kolb (2005) 'Conversation as Experiential Learning', *Management Learning* 36.4: 411-27.

Barrett, F.J., and R.E. Fry (2005) *Appreciative Inquiry* (Chargrin Falls, OH: Taos Institute Publications).

Bendell, J., I. Doyle, J. Cohen, E. Irwin and N. Black (2010) *Capitalism in Question: The Lifeworth Annual Review of Corporate Responsibility in 2009* (Lifeworth, www.lifeworth.com/capitalisminquestion.pdf).

Benyus, J. (2002) *Biomimicry: Innovation Inspired by Nature* (New York: Harper Perennial).

Blowfield, M., and B.K. Googins (2006) *Step Up: A Call for Business Leadership in Society. CEOs Examine the Role of Business in the 21st Century* (Chestnut Hill, MA: Boston College Centre for Corporate Citizenship).

Bornstein, D. (2007) *How to Change the World: Social Entrepreneurs and the Power of Ideas* (New York: Oxford University Press).

Brown, L. (2010) 'How to Feed 8 Billion People', *The Futurist*, January-February 2010: 28-33.

Brown, H.S., M. de Jong and T. Lessidrenska (2007) *The Rise of the Global Reporting Initiative (GRI) as a Case of Institutional Entrepreneurship,* (Cambridge, MA: John F. Kennedy School of Government, Harvard University, Corporate Social Responsibility Initiative, Working Paper No 36).

Brundtland Commission (1987) *Our Common Future* (Oxford, UK: Oxford University Press).

Cameron, K.S., J.E. Dutton and R.E. Quinn (eds.) (2003) *Positive Organisational Scholarship: Foundations of a New Discipline* (San Francisco, CA: Berrett-Koehler).

Capra, F. (1995) *The Web of Life* (New York: Anchor Doubleday).

Cavanagh, J., J. Mander, S. Anderson, D. Barker, M. Barlow, W. Bellow, R. Broad, T. Clarke, E. Goldsmith, R. Hayes, C. Hines, A. Kimbrell, D.Korten, H. Norberg-Hodge, S. Larrain, S. Retallack, V. Shiva, V. Tauli-Corpuz, and L. Wallch (2002) *Alternatives to Economic Globalisation* (San Francisco, CA: Berrett-Koehler).

Chandler, A.D. (1962) *Strategy and Structure* (Cambridge, MA: MIT Press).

Cheit, E.F. (1984) 'Business Schools and Their Critics', *California Management Review* 27.3: 43-62.

Christensen, C.M., H. Baumann, R. Ruggles and T.M. Stadtler (2006) 'Disruptive Innovation for Social Change', *Harvard Business Review*, December 2006: 94-101.

Churchman, C.W. (1967) 'Guest Editorial: Wicked Problems', *Management Science* 15.4: B141-42.

Clark, D., and M. McGillivray (2007) 'Measuring Human Wellbeing: Key Findings and Policy Lessons' (UNU Policy Brief, Volume 03/2007; United Nations University).

Collins, J.C. (2001) *Good to Great: Why Some Companies Make the Leap . . . and Others Don't* (New York: Collins Business).

—— and J.I. Porras (1997) *Built to Last: Successful Habits of Visionary Companies* (New York: Harper Business).

Commission on Human Security (2003) *Human Security Now* (New York: Commission on Human Security, www.humansecurity-chs.org/finalreport/index.html).

Costanza, R., M. Hart, S. Posner and J. Talbert (2009) 'Beyond GDP: The Need for New Measures of Progress' (The Pardee Papers 4; Boston University, January 2009).

Csikszentmihalyi, M. (1991) *Flow: The Psychology of Optimal Experience* (New York: HarperCollins).

—— (1997) *Finding Flow: The Psychology of Engagement with Everyday Life* (New York: Basic Books).

—— (1999) 'If We're So Rich, Why Aren't We Happy?', *American Psychologist* 54.10: 821-27.

Davis, G.F. (2009) *Managed by the Markets: How Finance Re-Shaped America* (New York: Oxford University Press).

Dawkins, R. (1976) *The Selfish Gene* (Oxford, UK: Oxford University Press).

Dees, G. (1998) *The Meaning of Social Entrepreneurship* (Chapel Hill, NC: Duke University, www.fuqua.duke.edu/centers/case/documents/dees_SE.pdf, 1998, rev. 2001).

Diamond, J. (2005) *Collapse: How Societies Choose to Fail or Survive* (New York: Viking Press).

Dichter, T. (2007) 'The Myth of Micro-finance', *Banker* 157. 1977: 10.

Donaldson, T., and T. Dunfee (1999) *Ties That Bind: A Social Contracts Approach to Business Ethics* (Boston, MA: Harvard Business School Press).

Emerson, J. (2003) 'The Blended Value Proposition: Integrating Social and Financial Returns', *California Management Review* 45.4: 35-45.

Erb-Leoncavallo, A.M. (2000) 'The Road from Seattle', *United Nations Chronicle* (online edition) XXXVII.1, www.wwan.cn/Pubs/chronicle/2000/issue1/0100p28.htm.

Ernst, C., and J. Yip (2009) 'Boundary Spanning Leadership: Tactics to Bridge Social Identity Groups in Organisations', in T. Pittinsky (ed.), *Crossing the Divide: Intergroup Leadership in a World of Difference* (Boston, MA: Harvard Business School Press).

Frederick, W.C. (1995) *Values, Nature and Culture in the American Corporation* (New York: Oxford University Press).

Freeman, R.E. (1984) *Strategic Management: A Stakeholder Approach* (Boston, MA: Pitman).

——, J. Harrison and A. Wicks (2007) *Managing for Stakeholders: Business in the 21st Century* (New Haven, CT: Yale University Press).

——, J. Harrison, A. Wicks, B. Parmar and S. de Colle (2010) *Stakeholder Theory: The State of the Art* (Oxford, UK: Oxford University Press).

Greenfield, K (2005) 'New Principles for Corporate Law', *Hastings Business Law Journal* 1 (May 2005): 87-118.

—— (2010a) 'A campaign funding mess', *Boston Globe*, 23 January 2010, www.boston.com/bostonglobe/editorial_opinion/oped/articles/2010/01/23/a_campaign_funding_mess.

—— (2010b) 'A way out of the Citizens United mess?' *The Huffington Post*, 22 January 2010, www.huffingtonpost.com/kent-greenfield/a-way-out-of-the-citizens_b_431990.html.

Guerrera, F. (2009) 'Welch rues short-term profit "obsession" ', *Financial Times*, 12 March 2009, us.ft.com/ftgateway/superpage.ft?news_id=fto031220091430053057.

Hagel, J., and J.F. Rayport (1997) 'The Coming Battle for Customer Information', *Harvard Business Review* 75.1: 53-65.

Handy, C. (2002) 'What's a Business for?', *Harvard Business Review*, December 2002: 49-55.

Hart, S. (1997) 'Beyond Greening: Strategies for a Sustainable World', *Harvard Business Review* 75.1: 66-76.

—— (2005a) *Capitalism at the Crossroads: The Unlimited Business Opportunities in Solving the World's Most Difficult Problems* (Philadelphia, PA: Wharton School Publishing).

—— (2005b) 'Innovation, Creative Destruction and Sustainability', *Research Technology Management* 48.5: 21-27.

Hawken, P. (1993) *The Ecology of Commerce* (New York: Harper Business).

—— (2008) *Blessed Unrest: How the Largest Movement in the World Came into Being and Why No One Saw It Coming* (New York: Viking Press).

——, A. Lovins and L. Hunter Lovins (1999) *Natural Capitalism: Creating the Next Industrial Revolution* (Boston, MA: Little Brown).

Hobsbawm, E. (2007) *Globalisation, Democracy and Terrorism* (Boston, MA: Little Brown).

Holliday, C., S. Schmidheiny and P. Watts. (2002) *Walking the Talk: The Business Case for Sustainable Development* (Sheffield, UK: Greenleaf Publishing)..

IEA (2008) *World Energy Outlook 2008: Executive Summary*, www.worldenergyoutlook.org/docs/weo2008/WEO2008_es_english.pdf.

IPCC (2007) *Fourth Assessment Report, Climate Change 2007: Synthesis Report*, www.ipcc.ch/pdf/assessment-report/ar4/syr/ar4_syr_spm.pdf.

Islam, N. (2009) 'Can Micro-finance Reduce Economic Insecurity and Poverty? By How Much and How?' DESA Working Paper No. 82 (St/ESA/2009/DWP/81, www.un.org/esa/desa/papers/2009/wp82_2009.pdf).

Jensen, M.C. (2000) 'Value Maximisation, Stakeholder Theory and the Corporate Objective Function', *Journal of Applied Corporate Finance* 14.3: 8-21.

Karnani, A. (2007) 'Mirage at the Bottom of the Pyramid: How the Private Sector Can Help Alleviate Poverty', *California Management Review* 49.4: 90-111.

Kegan, R. (1982) *The Evolving Self: Problem and Process in Human Development* (Cambridge, MA: Harvard University Press).

Kell, G., and J.G. Ruggie (1999) 'Global Markets and Social Legitimacy: The Case of the Global Compact', presented at *Governing the Public Domain Beyond the Era of the Washington Consensus? Redrawing the Line Between the State and the Market*, York University, Toronto, Canada, 4-6 November 1999, www.unglobalcompact.org/NewsandEvents/articles_and_papers/global_markets_social_legitimacy_york_university.html.

Keynes, J.M. (1932) 'Possibilities for Our Grandchildren'; www.econ.yale.edu/smith/econ116a/keynes1.pdf, accessed 13 April 2009.

Kohlberg, L. (1973) 'Stages and Ageing in Moral Development: Some Speculation', *The Gerontologist* 13.4: 497-502.

—— (1976) 'Moral Stages and Moralisation: The Cognitive-Developmental Approach', in T. Lickona, G. Geis and L.Kohlberg (eds.), *Moral Development and Behaviour: Theory, Research and Social Issues* (New York: Holt, Rinehart & Winston).

Ki-moon, B. (2009) 'The Global Compact: Creating Sustainable Markets', plenary speech at the World Economic Forum, Davos, 29 January 2009; www.unglobalcompact.org/docs/news_events/9.1_news_archives/2009_01_29b/unsg_davos2009.pdf.

Klein. N. (2007) *Shock Doctrine: The Rise of Disaster Capitalism* (New York: Metropolitan Books).

Korten, D. (2010) *Agenda for a New Economy: From Phantom Wealth to Real Wealth* (San Francisco: Berrett-Koehler, 2nd edn).

Krugman, P. (2009) 'How did economists get it so wrong?' *New York Times*, 6 September 2009, www.nytimes.com/2009/09/06/magazine/06Economic-t.html.

Liptak, A. (2010) 'Justices, 5-4, reject corporate spending limit', *New York Times*, 21 January 2010, www.nytimes.com/2010/01/22/us/politics/22scotus.html.

Lipton, B.H., and S. Bhaerman (2009) *Spontaneous Evolution: Our Positive Future and How to Get There* (New York: Hay House).

Louv, R. (2005) *Last Child in the Woods: Saving Our Children from Nature Deficit Disorder* (Conshohawken, PA: Atlantic Books).

Lydenberg, S. (2009) 'Beyond Risk: Notes Toward Responsible Alternatives for Investment Theory', Working Paper, Domini Social Funds; www.unpri.org/files/Lydenberg_PRI2009.pdf.

Martin, R.L., and S. Osberg (2007) 'Social Entrepreneurship: The Case for Definition', *Stanford Social Innovation Review*, Spring 2007: 29-38.

Matten, D., and A. Crane (2004) 'Corporate Citizenship: Towards an Extended Theoretical Conceptualisation', *Academy of Management Review* 29: 166-79.

McGann, J., and M. Johnstone (2006) 'The Power Shift and the NGO Credibility Crisis', *The International Journal of Not-for-Profit Law* 8.2 (www.icnl.org/KnoWleDge/ijnl/vol8iss2/art_4.htm#_ednref2).

McGillivray, M. (ed.) (2006) *Human Wellbeing: Concepts and Measurement* (Basingstoke, UK: Palgrave Macmillan).

McIntosh, M. (2008) 'Editorial', *Journal of Corporate Citizenship* 30 (Summer 2008).

——, R. Thomas, D. Leipziger and G. Coleman (2003) 'Learning from Company Engagement with the Global Compact', in *idem, Living Corporate Citizenship* (London: FT Prentice Hall).

McKeown, A., and G. Gardners (2009) *Climate Change Reference Guide* (Worldwatch Institute, www.worldwatch.org/files/pdf/CCRG.pdf).

McMichael, A.J., J.W. Powles, C.D. Butler and R. Uauy (2007) 'Food, Livestock Production, Energy, Climate Change and Health', *Lancet* 370: 1253-63.

Mirvis, P., and B. Googins (2006) 'Stages of Corporate Citizenship', *California Management Review* 48.2: 104-26.

Mont, O.K. (2002) 'Clarifying the Concept of Product-Service System', *Journal of Cleaner Production* 10: 237-45.

Morrison, J., M. Morikawa, M. Murphy and P. Schulte (2009) *Water Scarcity and Climate Change: Growing Risks for Businesses and Investors* (Ceres, www.ceres.org/Document.Doc?id=406).

Morgan, M. (2004) 'The Origins of the New Terrorism', *Parameters* (US Army War College Quarterly, www.carlisle.army.mil/usawc/parameters/04spring/morgan.pdf): 29-43.

Mulrow, J. (2009) 'Climate change proceeds down worrisome path', *Vital Signs*, 3 December 2009, vitalsigns.worldwatch.org/vs-trend/climate-change-proceeds-down-worrisome-path.

Murdoch, J. (1998) 'Does Micro-finance Really Help the Poor? New Evidence from Flagship Programmes in Bangladesh' (Princeton University Working Paper No. 198, ideas.repec.org/p/pri/rpdevs/198.html).

Nepstad, D.C. (2008) *The Amazon's Vicious Cycles* (WWF, assets.panda.org/downloads/amazonas_eng_04_12b_web.pdf).

New York Times (2009a) '200 Million and Counting', *New York Times*, 5 April 2009.

—— (2009b) 'Editorial: The Rights of Corporations', *New York Times*, 21 September 2009, www.nytimes.com/2009/09/22/opinion/22tue1.html?_r=1.

NIC (2008) *Global Trends 2025* (Washington, DC: National Intelligence Council, www.dni.gov/nic/PDF_2025/2025_Global_Trends_Final_Report.pdf).

Perkins, J. (2004) *Confessions of an Economic Hit Man* (San Francisco, CA: Berrett-Koehler).

—— (2007) *The Secret History of the American Empire: The Truth about Economic Hit Men, Jackals and the Truth about Global Corruption* (New York: Dutton).

—— (2009) *Hoodwinked: An Economic Hit Man Reveals Why the World Financial Markets Imploded—And What We Need to Do to Remake Them* (New York: Broadway Books).

Perman, S., J. Tozzi, A.S. Choi, A. Barrett, J. Quittner and N. Leiber (2009) 'America's most promising social entrepreneurs', *Business Week*, 3 April 2009, www.businessweek.com/smallbiz/content/mar2009/sb20090330_541747.htm.

Piazza, J.A. (2006) 'Rooted in Poverty? Terrorism, Poor Economic Development and Social Cleavages', *Terrorism and Political Violence* 18: 159-77.

Pollan, M. (2007) *The Omnivore's Dilemma: A Natural History of Four Meals* (New York: Penguin).

—— (2009a) *In Defence of Food: An Eater's Manifesto* (New York: Penguin).

—— (2009b) 'Farmer in chief', *New York Times*, 12 October 2009, www.scuolafattoria.it/documenti/cibo_politica.pdf.

Porritt, J. (2006) *Capitalism as if the World Matters* (London: Earthscan).

Post, J.E., L.E. Preston and S. Sachs (2002a) 'Managing the Extended Enterprise: The New Stakeholder View', *California Management Review* 45.1: 6-29;

——, L.E. Preston and S. Sachs (2002b) *Redefining the Corporation* (New York: Oxford University Press).

Prahalad, C.K. (2005) *The Fortune at the Bottom of the Pyramid: Eradicating Poverty Through Profits* (New Delhi, India: Pearson Education/Wharton School Publishing).

—— and A. Hammond (2002) 'Serving the World's Poor Profitably', *Harvard Business Review,*: 48-57.

Rees, S. (2003) *Passion for Peace* (Sydney, Australia: UNSW Press).

Rheingold, H. (2003) *Smart Mobs: The Next Social Revolution* (New York: Basic Books).

Rothenberg, S. (2007) 'Sustainability Through Servicising', *Sloan Management Review* 48.2: 83-91.

Ruggie, J. (2004) 'The Theory and Practice of Learning Networks', in M. McIntosh, S. Waddock and G. Kell (eds.), *Learning To Talk: Corporate Citizenship and the Development of the UN Global Compact* (Sheffield, UK: Greenleaf Publishing).

Sabati, H. (2009) *The Emerging Fourth Sector: Executive Summary* (Washington, DC: Aspen Institute, www.fourthsector.net).

Sainter, J. (1990) *The Collapse of Complex Societies* (Cambridge, UK: Cambridge University Press).

Salamon, L.M., S.W. Sokolowski and R. List (2003) *Civil Society: An Overview*, The Johns Hopkins Comparative Non-profit Sector Project, Centre for Civil Society Studies (Baltimore, MD: Johns Hopkins University, adm-cf.com/jhu/pdfs/Books/BOOK_GCS_2003.pdf).

Scherer, A.G., and G. Palazzo (2008) 'Globalisation and Corporate Social Responsibility', in A. Crane, A. McWilliams, D. Matten, J. Moon and D. Siegel (eds.), *The Oxford Handbook of Corporate Social Responsibility* (Oxford, UK Oxford University Press, ssrn.com/abstract=989565): 413-31.

——, G. Palazzo and D. Baumann (2006) 'Global Rules and Private Actors: Towards a New Role of the TNC in the Global Governance', *Business Ethics Quarterly* 16.4: 404-532.

Schumpeter, J.A. (1962) *Capitalism, Socialism and Democracy* (New York: Harper Perennial).

Senge, P. (1990) *The Fifth Discipline* (New York: Free Press).

——, B. Smith, S. Schley, J. Laur and N. Kruschwitz (2008) *The Necessary Revolution: How Individuals and Organisations Are Working Together to Create a Sustainable World* (Washington, DC: US Green Building Council).

Sinha, J. (2009) 'Scale vs scope: size does not guarantee success', *The Wall Street Journal*, 29 May 2009, www.livemint.com/2009/02/16204314/Scale-vs-Scope--Sizedoes-not.html.

Smith, A. (1776) *An Inquiry into the Nature and Causes of the Wealth of Nations* (London: W. Strahan and T. Cadell).

Soros, G. (1987) *The Alchemy of Finance* (New York: John Wiley).

Spindler, C. (1995) *The Man In The Ice* (London: Phoenix).

Stiglitz, D.J. (2009) 'Moving Beyond Market Fundamentalism to a More Balanced Economy', *Annals of Public and Cooperative Economics* 80.3: 345-60.

Stout, L.A. (2008) 'Why We Should Stop Teaching Dodge v. Ford', *Virginia Law & Business Review* 3.1: 163-76.

Strom, S. (2007) 'Businesses try to make money and save the world', *New York Times*, 6 May 2007, www.nytimes.com/2007/05/06/business/yourmoney/06fourth.html?_r=1&em&ex=1178769600&en=f898dbb3ee9240ab&ei=5087%0A.

Sugg, Z. (2008) 'Food Price Crisis Triggers Questions about Global Food Security', World Resources Institute, www.wri.org/stories/2008/04/food-price-crisis-triggers-questions-about-global-food-security.

Susskind, L.E., B.W. Fuller, M. Frenez and D. Fairman (2003) 'Multi-Stakeholder Dialogue at the Global Scale', *International Negotiation* 8: 235-66.

Tapscott, D., and D. Ticol (2003) *The Naked Corporation: How the Age of Transparency Will Revolutionise Business* (New York: Free Press).

Toffler, A. (1984) *Future Shock* (New York: Bantam).

—— (1990) *Power Shift: Knowledge, Wealth and Violence at the Edge of the 21st Century* (New York: Bantam Books).

Tol, R.J. (2009) 'The Economic Effects of Climate Change', *Journal of Economic Perspectives* 23.2.

Torbert, W.R., and associates (2004) *Action Inquiry: The Secret of Timely and Transforming Leadership* (San Francisco: Berrett-Koehler).

US EPA (Environmental Protection Agency) (2008) 'Electronic Waste Management in the United States: Approach 1' (EPA530-R-08-009, July 2008; www.epa.gov/osw/conserve/materials/ecycling/docs/app-1.pdf).

Waddell, S. (2010) *Global Action Networks: Creating Our Future Together* (Basingstoke, UK: Palgrave Macmillan).

Waddock, S. (2003) 'Learning from Experience: The UN Global Compact Learning Forum 2002', *Journal of Corporate Citizenship* 11 (Autumn 2003): 51-67.

—— (2008a) 'Building a New Institutional Infrastructure for Corporate Responsibility', *Academy of Management Perspectives* 22.3: 87-108.

—— (2008b) *The Difference Makers: How Social and Institutional Entrepreneurs Built the Corporate Responsibility Movement* (Sheffield, UK: Greenleaf Publishing).

—— (2009) *Leading Corporate Citizens: Vision, Values, Value-Added* (New York: McGraw-Hill, 3rd edn [1st published 2002]).

—— and M. McIntosh (2009) 'Beyond Corporate Responsibility: Implications for Management Development', *Business and Society Review* 114.3: 295-325.

Wallace, J. (2009) 'The Security Dimensions of Climate Change', *Worldwatch Institute 2009 State of the World: Into a Warming World* (New York: W.W. Norton).

Ward, B. (1966) *Spaceship Earth* (New York: Columbia University Press).

—— and R. Dubos (1972) *Only One Earth: The Care and Maintenance of a Small Planet* (New York: W.W. Norton).

Watkins, K. (2008) *Human Development Report, 2007/2008: Fighting Climate Change: Human Solidarity in a Divided World, Summary* (United Nations Development Programme, hdr.undp.org/en/media/HDR_20072008_Summary_English.pdf).

Weissman, R. (2001) 'Why we protest', *Washington Post*, 10 September 2001, www.commondreams.org/views01/0910-01.htm.

—— (2007) 'Corporate power since 1980', *Multinational Monitor*, 31 May 2007, www.multinationalmonitor.org/editorsblog/index.php?/archives/54-Corporate-Power-Since-1980.html.

—— (2010) 'Shed a tear for democracy', *Huffington Post*, 21 January 2010, www.huffingtonpost.com/robert-weissman/shed-a-tear-for-democracy_b_432079.html.

Wesselink, B., J. Bakkes, A. Best, F. Hinterberger and P. ten Brink (2007) 'Measurement Beyond GDP', paper presented at the *Beyond GDP: Measuring Progress, True Wealth and the Wellbeing of Nations Conference*, Brussels, Belgium, 19-29 November 2007.

White, A.L., M. Stoughton and L. Feng (1999) 'The Quiet Transition to Extended Product Responsibility', paper submitted to US Environmental Protection Agency, May 1999, www.p2pays.org/ref/17/16433.pdf.

Wilber, K. (1995) *Sex, Ecology, Spirituality: The Spirit of Evolution* (Boston, MA: Shambhala Publications).

—— (2002) *A Theory of Everything: An Integral Vision for Business, Politics, Science and Spirituality* (Boston, MA: Shambhala Publications).

Wild, L. (2006) *Strengthening Global Civil Society* (London: Institute for Public Policy Research, www.globalpolicy.org/ngos/intro/general/2006/04strengthening.pdf).

Worldwatch Institute (2004) 'The State of Consumption Today', *State of the World Report*, www.worldwatch.org/node/810.

Worm, B., E.B. Barbier, N. Beaumont, J.E. Duffy, C. Folke, B.S. Halpern, J.B.C. Jackson, H.K. Lotz, F.Micheli, S.R. Paulmbi, E.Sala, K.A. Selkoe, J.J. Stachowicz and R. Watson (2006) 'Impacts of Biodiversity Loss on Ocean Ecosystem Services', *Science* 314.5800: 787-90.

Yip, J., C. Ernst and M. Campbell (2009) *Boundary Spanning Leadership: Mission Critical Perspectives from the Executive Suite* (Centre for Creative Leadership, www.ccl.org/leadership/pdf/research/BoundarySpanningLeadership.pdf).

Index

About the authors

Sandra Waddock is Galligan Chair of Strategy and Professor of Management at Boston College's Carroll School of Management. Recent books include *The Difference Makers: How Social and Institutional Entrepreneurs Created the Corporate Responsibility Movement* (Greenleaf Publishing, 2008), *Leading Corporate Citizens: Vision, Values, Value Added* (Irwin Professional, 2005) and *Total Responsibility Management: The Manual* (with Charles Bodwell; Greenleaf Publishing, 2007). Author of over 100 papers on corporate responsibility, system change, collaboration, among other topics, Waddock was a co-founder of the Boston College Leadership for Change Program, the Institute for Responsible Investing, and the Business Ethics 100 Best Corporate Citizens ranking, and edited the *Journal of Corporate Citizenship* from 2003–2004. She received the 2004 Sumner Marcus Award for Distinguished Service from the Social Issues in Management Division of the Academy of Management, and the 2005 Faculty Pioneer Award for External Impact by Aspen Institute's Business in Society Program and the World Resources Institute. She was a visiting scholar at Harvard's Kennedy School of Government (2006–2007) and University of Virginia's Darden Graduate School of Business (2000).

Dr **Malcolm McIntosh** FRSA is Professor and Director of the Asia Pacific Centre for Sustainable Enterprise at Griffith University, Queensland, Australia, and is Visiting Professor of Human Security and Sustainable Enterprise in the Centre for Peace and Reconciliation, Coventry University, England; Visiting Professor, Department of Civil Engineering, University of Bristol, England; and Professor Extraordinaire, Sustainability Institute, Stellenbosch University, South Africa. He has previously worked at the Universities of Warwick, Bath and Coventry. Malcolm is Deputy Chair of the UN Global Compact Network Australia and has served as a Special Advisor to the UN Secretary-General's Global Compact in New York. He is a member of the PRME (Principles for Responsible Management Education) steering group and the Milan-based EABIS-funded GOLDEN for Sustainability council. He has served on the boards of AccountAbility, GRLI (Global Responsible Leaders Initiative), and the Bath-based Envolve partnerships for sustainability. His latest books are: *SEE Change: Making The Transition to the Sustainable Enterprise Economy* (with Sandra Waddock; Greenleaf Publishing, 2011) and *New Perspectives on Human Security* (edited with Alan Hunter; Greenleaf Publishing, 2010).

He has worked on sustainability, corporate responsibility and ethics issues for nearly 30 years building cross-sector partnerships for learning and co-creating a future founded on the principles of social justice, sustainability and organisational responsibility. Often overlapping he has had careers in business, peace research and the media, including working for BBC TV for ten years, part of the time in the Natural History Unit. He currently works in partnership with the UN University in Tokyo, the Eden Project in Cornwall, and various multinational companies and international NGOs around the world.